LAW EXPRESS: EXAM SUCCESS

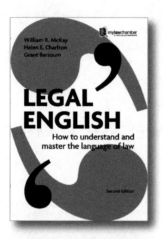

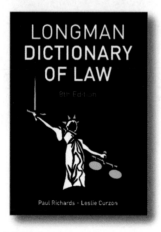
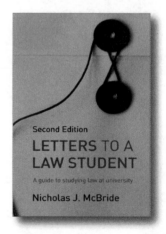

EXAM SUCCESS

Emily Finch
Stefan Fafinski

Longman
is an imprint of

Harlow, England • London • New York • Boston • San Francisco • Toronto • Sydney • Singapore • Hong Kong
Tokyo • Seoul • Taipei • New Delhi • Cape Town • Madrid • Mexico City • Amsterdam • Munich • Paris • Milan

Pearson Education Limited
Edinburgh Gate
Harlow
Essex CM20 2JE
England

and Associated Companies throughout the world

Visit us on the World Wide Web at:
www.pearson.com/uk

First edition 2012

ISBN: 978-1-4058-5947-9

British Library Cataloguing-in-Publication Data
A catalogue record for this book is available from the British Library

Library of Congress Cataloging-in-Publication Data
Finch, Emily.
  Law express : exam success / Emily Finch, Stefan Fafinski. -- 1st ed.
      p. cm. -- (Law express series)
  Includes index.
  ISBN 978-1-4058-5947-9 (pbk.)
  1. Law--Great Britain--Examinations, questions, etc. I. Fafinski, Stefan. II. Title. III. Title: Exam success.
  KD663.F56 2011
  340.076--dc23

                                        2011020152

10 9 8 7 6 5 4 3 2 1
14 13 12 11

Typeset in 10pt Helvetica Condensed by 3

Printed and bound in Great Britain by Henry Ling Ltd, Dorchester, Dorset

Contents

Supporting resources

Visit the Law Express: *Exam Success* companion website at **www.pearsoned.co.uk/lawexpress** to find valuable student learning material including:

- A downloadable revision calendar to help you plan and maintain your revision schedule
- Sample essay plans and problem question answers with examiner comments
- Examples of the activities mentioned in the text for you to try yourself
- An intelligence profile to discover your personal learning style
- A list of marking criteria to see what examiners are really looking for
- A downloadable exam checklist of essential things to remember before the exam
- Video clips featuring students sharing their personal experiences
- Instructions for doing a time audit with suggestions for eliminating time-wasting habits

Also: The companion website provides the following features:

- Search tool to help locate specific items of content
- E-mail results and profile tools to send results of quizzes to instructors
- Online help and support to assist with website usage and troubleshooting

For more information please contact your local Pearson Education sales consultant or visit **www.pearsoned.co.uk/lawexpress**

Acknowledgements

This book is dedicated to STG.

The authors would like to thank all those who have supported the development of this book for their helpful advice and comments, but with particular thanks to Christine Statham at Pearson.

We must also extend our gratitude to all the students who participated in our research and who gave us some very honest and frank insights into the views of students facing law exams today. Special thanks to those whose quotations appear in the book: David, Archana, Tom, Emily, Matt, Holly, Eloise, Lauren, Janet, Julianne, Dev and Will. Further thanks go to those anonymous lecturers who gave us their comments that are also used throughout the book.

Finally, to our friends who tried not to ask the 'Is it finished yet?' question as our first deadline came and went, but instead encouraged us towards completion: Johnno (obligatory), Peter Day, Penny Wallace and Dawn Hardiman.

EF and SF
Wokingham
January 2011

◼ Publisher's acknowledgements

Our thanks go to all reviewers who contributed to the development of this text, including students who participated in research and focus groups which helped to shape the series format.

Introduction

The *Law Express* series is designed to help you revise effectively on a subject by subject basis. However, students who used the series also told us that they needed a separate book (in a similar style to *Law Express*) dealing with revision and exams *specifically for law students*. Undergraduate law students are faced with a large burden of reading and memory work, probably more so than any other discipline. Many find it difficult to process all of this information successfully at exam time. Law exam results in the first and second year are also taken into account by law firms when deciding which graduates to take on both for work placements and training contracts. Examination assessment is still the preferred method of assessment for law degrees, and many universities are moving away from coursework assessment as a result of increasing problems with plagiarism. Therefore there is a heavy burden for success in exams facing the majority of law students combined with a real need for support in how to perform in exams.

This book is a companion to the *Law Express* series. Our aim in writing it was to provide a guide to exam success in law and to help all students achieve their personal best. It will allow you to assess and address your particular weaknesses in revising, preparing for and succeeding in law exams and delivers tips, techniques and strategies to enable you to significantly improve your abilities and performance in time to make a difference. It focuses on particular concerns facing law students, such as what cases should be memorised and how, how to handle problem questions, how best to use statutes books and materials allowed into the exam hall, how to tackle different types of examination papers and how to select questions to answer from the paper. After the first chapter, which looks at different types of law exam and invites you to reflect upon your personal learning style, the book is split into two parts; the first dealing with the process of revision and the second dealing with the exam itself. Throughout the book you will also find quotations from real students and lecturers expressing their views from either side of the exam process. We hope that you find it useful and, on the assumption that you have acquired the book because you have law exams approaching, we wish you the very best of luck.

Emily Finch
Stefan Fafinski

Guided tour

Exam tips – Feeling the pressure? These boxes indicate how you can improve your exam performance and your chances of getting those top marks!

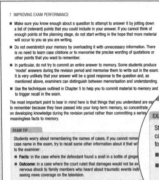

7 IMPROVING EXAM PERFORMANCE

■ Make sure you know enough about a question to attempt to answer it by jotting down a list of (relevant) points that you could include in your answer. If you cannot think of enough points at the planning stage, do not start writing in the hope that more material will occur to you as you are writing.

■ Do not overstretch your memory by overloading it with unnecessary information. There is no need to learn case citations or to memorise the precise wording of quotations or other points that you want to remember.

■ In particular, do not try to commit an entire answer to memory. Some students produce 'model' answers during the revision period and memorise them to write out in the exam. It is very unlikely that your answer will be a good response to the question and, as mentioned above, examiners can distinguish between memorisation and understanding.

■ Use the techniques outlined in Chapter 5 to help you to commit material to memory and to trigger recall in the exam.

The most important point to bear in mind here is that things that you understand are easy to remember because they have passed into your long-term memory, so concentrate on developing knowledge during the revision period rather than committing a series of meaningless facts to memory.

EXAM TIP

Students worry about remembering the names of cases. If you cannot remember a case name in the exam, try to recall some other information about it that will be useful to the examiner:

■ **Facts**: in the case where the defendant found a snail in a bottle of ginger...

■ **Outcome**: in a case where the court ruled that damages would not be available for nervous shock to family members who heard about traumatic events indirectly from seeing news coverage on the television.

■ **Judge**: in a case where Lord Bridge considered the relationship between European law and Parliamentary sovereignty.

Mismatch between question and answer

Your answer must be a perfect match to the question. Every question has parameters. In other words, an essay question is not simply about a particular topic but instead it asks you to discuss some specific point about that topic. Similarly, a problem question is designed to prompt an analysis of particular areas of law and not others. In order to create an answer that is a perfect match to the question, you must identify the focus of the question and select only material relevant for this focus for inclusion so that you make all the points that the question needs without discussing anything irrelevant.

96

EXAM TIP

Students worry about remembering the names of case... case name in the exam, try to recall some other informa... to the examiner:

■ **Facts**: in the case where the defendant found a snail...

■ **Outcome**: in a case where the court ruled that dama... nervous shock to family members who heard about... seeing news coverage on the television.

■ **Judge**: in a case where Lord Bridge considered... law and Parliamentary sovereignty.

Lecturer viewpoint – Ever wonder what your examiner is thinking? Get the inside perspective and hear straight from those who know about achieving exam success!

WHAT NOT TO DO

■ Go through various journal articles on the topic and agree the key points from each of them. Make lists of similarities and differences between alternative academic viewpoints.

Finally, it is important to remember that if you get to a point where you are collectively stuck, then you should seek help from your lecturer who should be willing to assist.

Lecturer viewpoint

I always like questions that come from study groups. If a group of students still don't get a topic after working together, then it might mean that I didn't explain it clearly enough in the lectures or that it might need more focus in tutorials. This feedback helps me make my course better for the next year, so of course I'll try to sort their problem out.

What not to do

There are some common pitfalls that can occur when working in a group:

■ **Neglecting your own study.** You need to make sure that you strike a balance between the needs of your own private study and supporting the other members of the study group. Make sure that you get as much out of the group as you put in. Working in a study group is not a soft option or an alternative to taking responsibility for your own learning.

■ **Bringing each other down.** Be careful not to let the session degenerate into a discussion of how difficult things are, your negative perceptions of the course, your lecturers or your fellow students. If you get a sense that this is happening, try to snap the rest of the group out of it and channel your energies into doing something positive.

■ **Wasting time.** Sometimes it is easier to chat about almost anything rather than studying. You need to focus on what you are trying to achieve together.

To find out more ... www.pearsoned.co.uk/lawexpress

Visit the Companion Website where you will find some further accounts from students about their experiences – good and bad – of revision as part of a group, along with tips for a successful revision group. You might find these useful when organising your own revision groups.

61

...e lists of similarities an...
...nts.

...y, it is important to remember that if you get t...
...ck, then you should seek help from your lecturer w...

Lecturer viewpoint

I always like questions that come from study groups. If a... get a topic after working together, then it might mean tha... enough in the lectures or that it might need more focus i... helps me make my course better for the next year, so of... problem out.

What not to do

...ome common pitfalls that can oc...
...wn study. Y...

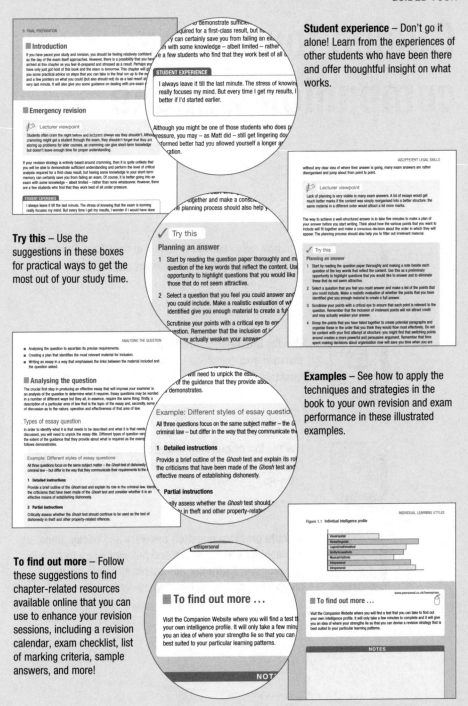

Student experience – Don't go it alone! Learn from the experiences of other students who have been there and offer thoughtful insight on what works.

Try this – Use the suggestions in these boxes for practical ways to get the most out of your study time.

Examples – See how to apply the techniques and strategies in the book to your own revision and exam performance in these illustrated examples.

To find out more – Follow these suggestions to find chapter-related resources available online that you can use to enhance your revision sessions, including a revision calendar, exam checklist, list of marking criteria, sample answers, and more!

Guided tour of the companion website

Practical resources are available to download. Print your own **exam checklist** and **revision calendar**!

Use the **intelligence profile** prior to your revision to discover your particular learning patterns and devise an effective revision strategy tailored to your strengths.

Use the **list of marking criteria** to understand what your examiner is looking for and to evaluate your own practice answers.

Sample problem question answers and **essay plans** are available for you to critique and put your exam technique into practice. **Examiner comments** give you the inside perspective on how to earn top marks.

Find examples of the **revision activities** and **strategies** outlined in the book for you to try yourself and prepare for exam success.

 Find instructions for doing a **time audit** and suggestions for eliminating your worst time-wasting habits.

 Watch **video clips** featuring students sharing their personal experiences and hard-won advice for facing exams with confidence.

All of this and more can be found when you visit
www.pearsoned.co.uk/lawexpress

Law exams
and you

1

Revision checklist

Topics covered in this chapter:

☐ Understanding the purpose of exams

☐ Types of law exams: open and closed book, seen and unseen exams

☐ Different types of questions: essays, problems, case notes, short answer questions

☐ Individual learning styles and their impact on revision

■ Introduction

The first step towards achieving success in exams is to understand their purpose. Once you appreciate what it is that exams are designed to test, you will be able to tailor your revision to ensure that you enter the exam room equipped to produce answers that satisfy the requirements of the exam and impress your examiners. This chapter starts by explaining the purpose of exams and moves on to outline the different formats of exam that you might encounter and the types of question that may arise with tips on how to tackle them. The final section of this chapter explains the different types of intelligence that exist and how this might affect the way that you approach revision.

■ The purpose of exams

The easiest way to explain the purpose of exams as a method of assessment is to draw an analogy with two unrelated situations: a medical examination and a sporting event.

- The purpose of a medical examination is for the doctor to assess whether the patient has a particular condition and, if so, how far it has developed. In other words, it establishes the presence and extent of a disease. Similarly, the purpose of an exam is to determine the presence and extent of the candidate's legal knowledge.

- A parallel can be drawn between exams and a big sporting event. After months of preparation, competitors/students are tested to see which of them is able to produce the most impressive performance under pressure. This allows competitors/students to be ranked in order of the quality of their performance.

In essence, then, the purpose of the exams is to determine how much each student knows about each particular area of law to enable the university to make a distinction between students on the basis of their knowledge and ability.

However, many students do not understand the value of exams as a method of assessment:

STUDENT EXPERIENCE

I hate exams. I can't see the point of them. All you do is memorise things from a book and regurgitate it in the exam. It isn't a test of knowledge, just of memory and that is pointless because solicitors and barristers aren't expected to remember the law, they just look it up. They're also unfair because most students end up with much worse marks than they do for their coursework.

Matt

This quotation sums up three of the commonest criticisms that students make about the use of exams as a method of assessment in law:

- Exams are a test of memory rather than a means of measuring knowledge.
- Their emphasis on the ability to memorise the law is irrelevant to the reality of legal practice.
- Exams are more challenging and result in lower marks for most students.

Although these views are commonly held, they are inaccurate, as will be explained in the sections that follow.

Memory *versus* knowledge

Exams are not designed to be a test of memory: their purpose is to test knowledge. The brain processes and stores information differently depending upon whether or not it has been understood. If you understand an area of law, it is stored in the brain as knowledge where it takes up less room and can be more easily retrieved than law which has not been understood but which has been committed to memory. This means that students who have memorised law that they do not understand have far fewer resources to draw upon in the exam than students who have understood the law and have far more detailed knowledge stored in their brain.

Students often equate memory and knowledge, thinking that the ability to remember and reproduce accurate statements of the law is a method of demonstrating knowledge. However, examiners are looking for answers that show understanding of the law rather than answers that are made up of points that have been memorised. Understanding is expressed by an ability to explain the law in your own words and to use it in a flexible way to respond to the requirements of the question. Students who are relying on memorised information tend to struggle to produce answers with either of these characteristics.

 Lecturer viewpoint

There is a qualitative difference between answers based on understanding of the law and those that are made up of a series of memorised points. The latter attract very little credit.

So although the importance of remembering the law that you have learned might make it seem as if exams are all about memory, this is not the case. Do not use memorisation as a substitute for knowledge. The two things are very different and the distinction is highly visible to examiners.

Academic law *versus* law in practice

Whilst it is true that lawyers in practice are not expected to work from memory, it is important to remember that a law degree is not designed to prepare students for practice or to replicate the conditions in which solicitors and barristers work. The academic study of the law is intended to provide a general grounding in the law and, like other academic subjects, exams are used as one of the main methods of assessment.

Although law is studied as an academic discipline at undergraduate level, the use of exams as a method of assessment makes a positive contribution to equipping students to enter into legal practice. One of the key pedagogic justifications for the use of unseen exams (that is, exams where the questions are not released to students prior to their entry into the exam room) is that it stimulates and motivates student learning across the entire syllabus of any particular subject. In other words, students do not know what topics will be examined so the sensible approach to revision to ensure preparedness for the exam is to revise a significant proportion of the material covered in each module. By way of comparison, assessment by coursework requires a sustained focus on a single topic, so does not promote breadth of knowledge in the same way as assessment by exam.

Exams *versus* coursework

Many students do find that they receive lower marks for exams than for coursework. This should not be taken to mean that exams are harder than coursework, but that each method of assessment sets out to test different things and students are better at meeting the objectives of coursework.

STUDENT EXPERIENCE

I used to think that I was much better at coursework than exams as my marks were about 10–15 per cent better in coursework. Then I realised that the way that I approached exams was wrong so I made a lot of changes to the way that I revised and now my marks are pretty much the same for exams and coursework.

Louise

There would be no point in having two methods of assessment if coursework and assessment had the same objectives and tested students in the same way.

■ Types of law exam

The sections that follow will introduce the various types of exam that you might encounter and provide some guidance on how to adapt your approach to revision to suit their requirements.

Seen and unseen exams

The most usual method of assessment in undergraduate law is the unseen paper. This is an exam in which students do not have any advance knowledge about the topics that will be examined and the questions that will be asked about them. This can be distinguished from a seen exam (also known as a pre-release paper) in which the paper is given to students prior to the exam to enable them to prepare with full knowledge of the questions.

Preparing for a seen exam

Clearly, the business of revising for an exam will differ dramatically depending upon whether you are preparing for a seen or unseen paper. Knowledge of the questions prior to the exam facilitates targeted revision and enables students to focus their attention on the topics that are certain to appear on the paper. Students preparing for a seen exam paper not only have an opportunity to tailor their revision to the content of the exam but are also able to carry out research and plan their answers. All that is required is that this information is retained until the exam, as it is generally the case that materials are not permitted into the exam room. A final point to remember about a seen exam paper is the examiners will expect a higher standard of answer as students have had advance knowledge of the questions.

Preparing for an unseen exam

By contrast, preparation for an unseen paper is speculative and necessitates that students revise more topics than there are questions to be answered to ensure that they will be able to answer the required number of questions. A student who revises four topics in preparation for an unseen exam paper that requires that four questions are answers runs a risk of being caught out if one (or more) of their topics does not come up on the paper or the question asked about the topic is one that they cannot tackle.

Open and closed book exams

The most usual method of assessment in undergraduate law is the closed book exam. In this style of exam, students are not permitted to take any materials into the exam room to consult when preparing their answers (except perhaps a statute book). By contrast, students sitting an open book exam are permitted to take materials into the exam room and use these in preparing their answers. This may be a single book determined by the examiner, your own choice of one book or you may have the option of taking as many books as you choose into the exam. Some open book exams require students to write their own notes to take into the exam instead of a textbook.

Preparing for an open book exam

An open book exam might seem like a very easy option, both in terms of preparation and actually answering the questions in the exam, as you may feel that the presence of the book relieves you of the need to revise beforehand as you can simply look up the information that you need. This is a mistake.

 Lecturer viewpoint

Watching students in an open book exam can be painful. I see students burning up far too much time searching for the information that they want and students copying pages of detail out of the textbook onto their exam paper. I think that an open book exam presents students with so many ways to go wrong that it is often much harder to tackle than a closed book exam.

Anything that makes it easier for you to find the information that you want amongst the hundreds of pages of the book will be of great value to you in the pressure of the exam. Check the rules that govern the exam to see if you are permitted to annotate the book, to highlight it or to use sticky tabs to help you find your way around the book.

STUDENT EXPERIENCE

I was conscious of the need to be able to find things quickly in the exam so I devised a simple system of colour coding: blue for case names, pink for quotations, green for statutes, purple for definitions and yellow for other important points.

Julianne

If you are preparing for an open book exam, the best piece of advice that you could possibly receive would be to revise as if it were a closed book exam and to try, as far as you are able, only to refer to the book as briefly as possible when answering questions in the exam.

Preparing for a closed book exam

A closed book exam is a more traditional test of your ability to retrieve relevant knowledge so requires a combination of understanding and memory. As this is the most common exam format that you are likely to encounter during your undergraduate studies, the bulk of the advice in this book is aimed at equipping you with guidance on preparing for a closed book exam.

■ Types of question

Essays and problem questions are by far the most common types of questions that appear on exam papers in law. In fact, many students may not encounter any other kind of question during their undergraduate studies. Chapters 8 and 9 provide detailed guidance on all aspects of writing essays and answering problem questions in exams so the sections that follow will provide only a basic outline of their characteristics whilst dealing with other, less usual, types of question in more detail.

Essay questions

Discussion and analysis are the key words to remember when writing an essay. The commonest weakness of essays produced in exam conditions is that they focus too much on describing the subject matter of the question and do too little – sometimes nothing at all – to engage with the line of discussion required by the question.

> **EXAM TIP**
>
> Look at the slant of the question – it may present a viewpoint or invite an opinion – and take a stance on it. Design your line of argument to present this stance, remembering to take account of opposing views where appropriate.

Problem questions

A problem question is a hypothetical set of facts that gives rise to a legal dispute that requires that you give advice to one or more party about the viability of their claim or the strength of the claim against them.

The skill at the heart of successful problem solving is the application of the law to the facts. This is a skill that should be practised and honed prior to the exam so that it is second nature by the time that you reach the exam room.

Case notes and commentaries

A case note or case commentary tests your ability to pick particular pieces of information out of a case in order to analyse it. The approach to creating a case note or commentary tends to vary a little between different universities but the key information that you might be expected to identify is as follows:

■ **Material facts.** The ability to distinguish between the material facts (those that are significant in framing the legal issue) from the mass of detail within the case is a key skill.

- **Legal issues.** What point of law was the court addressing? This may be spelt out explicitly in the case or you may have to work it out.

- **Judicial background.** You may be required to outline the history of the appeal and summarise findings of the earlier courts.

- **Outcome.** State whether the appeal was upheld or rejected, taking care to note whether it was a majority decision.

- ***Ratio decidendi* and *obiter dicta*.** Ensure that you are able to distinguish between the *ratio* of the case (the reason for the decision that is binding in subsequent cases) and things that are said *obiter* (in passing) by the judge that might nonetheless be significant.

- **Significant quotations.** You may be required to pick out particular quotes that demonstrate the reasoning of the court or which highlight certain features of the case.

- **Commentary.** This is the most challenging aspect of creating a case note as you are required to discuss the significance of the case and highlight its contribution to the development of the law as well as speculating about its potential impact.

In some universities, students are not given advance notice of the case that will be the subject of a commentary and are provided with a hitherto unseen case in the exam room. This precludes any possibility of preparation in terms of studying the case itself but you should practise your case-noting skills in the build up to the exam if you are aware that this type of question will appear on the paper. The more case notes you produce, the more skilful you will become at tracking down relevant information in the case. The alternative approach is that students are told that a particular case will be the focus of a commentary in the exam or that one case from a short list of cases will be used. This does provide an opportunity to study the case in advance of the exam so make sure that you are very familiar with the judgment and can identify the key points needed in the case note. It is also a very good idea to read around the case to find inspiration for points that you could include in the commentary section.

> **STUDENT EXPERIENCE**
>
> We were given a list of five cases and told that we would have to write a case note on one of them in the exam. Everyone was just reading the cases but I did a lot of research on the cases and read articles written about them so that I had a lot to say in the discussion section.
>
> *Eloise*

Short answer questions

As the title suggests, these are questions that require only a short response. It is an approach that is often used to assess your familiarity with key terms or significant cases that you have encountered in a particular module.

Example: Short answer questions

The following are two examples of the types of short answer question that you might encounter. In the first example, there is a single question on an exam paper that asks students to discuss key terms taken from across the module. This is likely to be the only question of its kind on an exam paper and will usually appear in conjunction with the usual mix of essays and problem questions. The second example shows a different approach in which the entire paper is made up of short answer questions about a range of issues within the module.

Key terms

Select four terms from the following list, explain their meaning and discuss their role and significance.

- Appropriation
- Virtual certainty
- Disease of the mind
- *Novus actus interveniens*
- More than merely preparatory
- Objective recklessness

Mixed questions

1 Explain the role of equity and identify at least two ways in which it differs from statute and case law. (4 marks)
2 Identify three differences between civil and criminal law. (3 marks)
3 Provide a brief explanation of alternative dispute resolution and comment on its benefits. (5 marks)
4 What is the rule in *Young* v. *Bristol Aeroplane*? (3 marks)

You might think that short answer questions are an easier option that an essay or a problem question. It is true that each answer requires less detail and it is a more straightforward task to write a paragraph on a topic than it is to construct a line of argument in an essay or untangle the facts in a problem question. However, the challenge of short answer questions is their breadth of coverage. As you see in the example above, both approaches draw their questions from across the syllabus; the key terms are taken from Criminal Law and the mixed questions are from an English Legal System module. This means that students have to be familiar with the entire syllabus in order to be able to tackle all the questions.

> **EXAM TIP**
>
> Short answer questions require good time-management. Work out how much time is available for each question by dividing the duration of the exam by the number of questions: for example, 30 questions in a two-hour exam works out at four minutes for each question. Of course, you may need to adjust this if some questions carry more marks than others.

Multiple choice questions

Multiple choice questions are not widely used in undergraduate law exams as they tend to be regarded as too straightforward and do not test the ability to reason or analyse the law. However, they are actually quite a good method of testing knowledge, so you may encounter a multiple choice section as one part of an exam paper.

The important point to remember about multiple choice questions is that they are not necessarily easy just because you do not have to generate the answer yourself but instead choose the correct answer from the range of options provided. A well-designed multiple choice question will create responses that are hard to differentiate thus requiring very precise knowledge of the law. If you do encounter multiple choice questions, do not make the mistake of underestimating their challenge.

■ Individual learning styles

Learning styles are different approaches to learning. Individual learning styles explain why some students only understand information when it is explained to them in a lecture whilst others need to read the same points in a textbook in order for them to make sense. It is useful to understand your own learning style as it can be really valuable in ensuring that you tailor your approach to revision to play to your strengths.

There are various ways of categorising learning styles, but one of the most popular is the multiple intelligence approach devised by an American developmental psychologist called Howard Gardner who outlined seven types of intelligence, as shown in Table 1.1.

Type	Characteristics	Revision activities
Visual/spatial intelligence	An ability to perceive concepts and take in information that is expressed visually. Ability to retain and recall information is associated with mental visualisation.	Students who are strong in visual/spatial intelligence should try visual means of presenting material such as diagrams, flow charts and mind maps. They may also find that memory is triggered by images and an ability to visualise themselves at a particular place so try to create links between location and particular revision topics.
Verbal/linguistic intelligence	Well able to use words and language. Think in words rather than pictures.	Students who are strong in verbal/linguistic intelligence should be skilled at using language persuasively. The focus should be reading and listening to take in information. People with this sort of intelligence are usually articulate speakers, so try recording your notes or explaining your understanding to others during the revision period.
Logical/mathematical intelligence	Ability to use reason and logic. Good at categorising information and making connections between pieces of information.	Students with a high level of logical/mathematical intelligence are logical and systematic workers so should do well at answering problem questions. Revision activities involving ordering and making connections between pieces of information will be particularly productive.
Bodily/kinaesthetic intelligence	Skilful at activities requiring movement and coordination. Good hand-eye coordination.	Students possessed of this form of intelligence have the ability to process and remember information by interacting with the space around them so should strive to make associations between place and revision topics. People with bodily/kinaesthetic intelligence tend to learn better by doing things rather than by more passive means so be sure to incorporate plenty of practice answers into your revision.

▶

Musical/rhythmic intelligence	Characterised by the ability to produce and appreciate music. Particularly prone to distraction from environmental sounds such as noise from building works or the ticking of a clock.	Make the most of this type of intelligence by creating links between revision topics and particular songs or types of music to aid recall. Students with musical/rhythmic intelligence can find their ability to concentrate is enhanced by the presence of music. Information can be made more memorable by the use of rhythm or rhyme. Be sure to find a work environment that is quiet to avoid the distraction of background sounds.
Interpersonal intelligence	Skilled in relating to others and understanding other's point of view and feelings.	Students strong in interpersonal intelligence often have good organisational skills which will be useful when revising. They are great people to have in a group, having excellent communication skills and being skilled at encouraging cooperation amongst group members. The ability to look at a situation from different perspectives could be useful in answering problem questions.
Intrapersonal intelligence	Ability to self-reflect. Able to evaluate their own performance and identify strengths and weaknesses.	Students with good intrapersonal skills are able to recognise and work towards their goals effectively. They are also skilled at recognising their own strengths and weaknesses which will be useful in selecting revision topics and activities to suit their abilities.

Table 1.1 Different types of intelligence

Do you recognise any of these characteristics in yourself? Perhaps you have always wondered why you work more effectively with music playing in the background but are distracted by the ticking of a clock: this could be due to high levels of musical/rhythmic intelligence. It may be that you find it very difficult to commit your revision notes to memory unless you create a mind map, in which case it is likely that this is due to your visual/spatial intelligence.

People do not have a single type of intelligence to the exclusion of all others but have a unique intelligence profile composed of all seven forms of intelligence in varying quantities as Figure 1.1 illustrates.

Figure 1.1 Individual intelligence profile

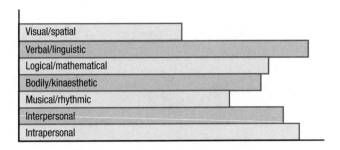

www.pearsoned.co.uk/lawexpress

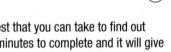

■ To find out more …

Visit the Companion Website where you will find a test that you can take to find out your own intelligence profile. It will only take a few minutes to complete and it will give you an idea of where your strengths lie so that you can devise a revision strategy that is best suited to your particular learning patterns.

NOTES

NOTES

Revision

Revision planning

Revision checklist

Topics covered in this chapter:

- [ ] Gathering information about the format and content of the exams
- [ ] Getting together revision materials
- [ ] Creating a good working environment that is free from distraction
- [ ] Planning revision taking into account the time available and working preferences
- [ ] Selecting revision topics
- [ ] Creating a revision timetable

■ Introduction

It is often said that 'failing to prepare is preparing to fail'. It would be unreasonable to suggest that students who do not carry out revision preparation are going to fail their exams but this chapter will argue that careful planning and preparation will give you a more structured and effective approach to revision. An organised approach may also make you feel more in control of your revision thus reducing feelings of stress in the build up to the exams. This chapter will outline a variety of techniques that will help you to plan your revision.

■ Preliminary matters

Before you can start to plan your revision, it is essential that you ensure that you have a clear idea of what it is you are working towards. This requires more than knowing the date and time of the first exam; you should be able to answer the following questions:

- What subjects are being examined?
- What is the date of each exam?
- How long is the exam?
- How many questions are there on each subject paper?
- Are there any compulsory questions?
- Do you have any information about the topics that will or will not be covered in each subject?
- Have you been told anything about the types of question; for example, is it a mix of essays and problems?
- Can you take any materials, such as a statute book, into the exam?

If you cannot answer all of these questions at the start of the revision period, you should make it your first task to track down this information. You might find that it is useful to enter this information into a table which you can then print out and keep somewhere visible for reference during the revision period.

	Contract	Criminal law	English legal systems	Public law
Date of exam	20th May	26th May	27th May	1st June
Length of exam	3 hours	3 hours	2 hours	3 hours
Number of questions	4	3	3	3
Time per question	45 minutes	1 hour	45 minutes	1 hour
Compulsory questions?	No but must answer one question from each part.	No	No	Yes
Topics covered or not covered	No info	No questions on insanity or intoxication.	There is a problem question on statutory interpretation.	The compulsory question is on judicial review. The coursework topic (tribunals) is not in the exam.
Type of questions	Part 1 has four essays and Part 2 has four problem questions. Must answer one from each part.	Free choice from a mix of eight essays and problem questions.	Free choice from two problem questions and eight essays.	No info but likely to be a mix of essays and problem questions.
Statute book?	Yes	Yes	No	No

As you can see, the table provides a useful reference point from which you can pick out key information about each exam that will enable you to make informed decisions about the topics and skills that need to be the focus of the revision period.

For example, a student facing the exams detailed above can take the following into account when planning their revision:

■ Their revision topics must include judicial review and statutory interpretation but exclude intoxication, insanity and tribunals. This is at least a starting point in terms of topic choice.

■ The time available to answer a question varies between exams so they will need to know topics in greater depth in Criminal Law and Public Law and they should practise writing answers in the two different time frames as part of their revision. The importance of writing practice answers is covered in Chapter 3.

■ As statute books are only permitted in two exams, different strategies are needed. Revision of Criminal Law and Contract should include navigation of statute books whilst revision for English Legal Systems and Public Law exams should include identifying and memorising some key statutory provisions (see Chapter 5).

■ As the Criminal Law paper requires that students answer at least one essay and one problem question, revision should take into account the skills sets involved with each type of question (see Chapters 8 and 9).

■ Preparing to revise

In order to prepare for revision, you should make sure that you have all the resources that you need to be able to revise effectively. This involves gathering together all the materials that you need and also ensuring that you have at least one suitable place to work where you can concentrate free from interruptions. It is worth taking time to think about these issues prior to starting your revision as it will really break your concentration if you have to go out to track down an article in the library or make adjustments to your working environment once your revision is underway.

Materials

You will need a range of different materials during the revision period. If you spend some time checking to ensure that you have everything that you need from the following list, it will save you time later as you should have all the materials that you need on hand:

■ **A complete set of notes for each subject.** Did you miss any lectures or fail to make notes for seminars? Gaps in your notes are often a sign of gaps in knowledge, so think carefully about whether you need to fill in the gaps or whether your time would be better spent consolidating your understanding of topics that you have already covered.

■ **A textbook that writes in a way that you find accessible.** It is sometimes the case that the set text that you bought at the beginning of the academic year just does not work for you. Perhaps it is a bit simplistic and you would like more depth or perhaps it is heavy going and you would prefer something a little easier to read. Your revision can be made so much easier if you are working with books that suit you, so explore what the library has to offer, making sure that the books that you choose are sufficiently up-to-date.

■ **Past exam papers for each of your subjects.** These are an invaluable revision resource because they give you information about the way that the exam is organised and the sorts of questions that you might encounter, which you can use for practice answers. However, you should check with a lecturer to ensure that the format of the exam has not changed.

■ **A statute book if you are permitted to take one into the exam room.** It is a good idea to use the revision period to ensure that you are familiar with the layout of the statute book and that you can find the relevant pieces of legislation quickly. You should also familiarise yourself with the rules relating to the use of statute books at your institution: most universities do not allow books to be used if there is writing in them, but there is less uniformity about highlighting and the use of sticky notes to mark pages.

■ **A selection of leading cases and relevant articles.** These will help you to gain a greater depth of understanding of the topics that you revise and the ability to incorporate these sources in your answer will impress your examiners (see the comment below). If you find it difficult to identify key cases and useful reading, you might find it helpful to look at the Law Express series which highlights this information for you.

 Lecturer viewpoint

I'm always impressed when I read an exam paper that has references to points made by particular judges in a leading case or when the student has made correct reference to an argument put forth by an academic. It says to me 'this is someone who has gone the extra mile and put some real effort into gaining knowledge of this topic'. And, of course, knowledge of those points enables the student to engage with the issues in greater depth which, in turn, leads to better marks.

Working environment

Where do you do your revision? For many students, their revision takes place at one location and this is the same place that they carry out the majority of their work during the course of their studies. This can be positive. For many people, having a set place where they study means that they can slip easily into work mode as soon as they sit down and this helps them to revise effectively. However, it is important to bear in mind that revision is different from the sort of studying that you usually do when you are making notes and preparing coursework. It requires more concentration as you try to digest a large volume of material and commit it to memory, so it may be that your usual work environment is not the most suitable place for you to carry out your revision.

Students at a revision workshop identified the following as the most important characteristics of a good revision environment:

- It should be comfortable. This included the temperature of the room and having space to get up and walk around.
- It should have everything that is needed for revision readily to hand. This included access to materials, having sufficient paper for notes and the ease of getting refreshments.
- It must be quiet and free from interruptions and distractions.

These factors may seem obvious, but it was surprising how many students said that their own revision environment did not deliver on all three elements. Think about whether your revision venue has these characteristics and, if it does not, consider ways of making improvements.

Have you ever thought about revising in different places? Not only will a different venue help you to avoid the distractions of your usual study environment but it can help in the process of recalling information that is stored in your memory as you make the link between a particular topic and the place in which you revised it.

STUDENT EXPERIENCE

I revise every topic in a different place: my room, the kitchen, my nan's house, the garden, the park, the library. All my friends sit in their rooms and revise so they think I'm mad but it really works for me because I associate the topic with the place I revised it so in the exam I can visualise myself sitting on a bench in the park and it all floods back to me.

David

Another reason that students have suggested in favour of different revision venues is that it can be a way to put time constraints on the time spent revising.

STUDENT EXPERIENCE

I was sitting at my desk all day and not making enough progress. It was meaningless to set myself a deadline of finishing by 6pm because I knew that if I wasn't finished I could keep going. I started going to the library three hours before it shut and that seemed to concentrate my mind. I got more done in those three hours than I did in a whole day of sitting at my desk.

David

You will find further discussion on the link between place and memory in Chapter 5.

Try this

Carry out a time audit

Give particular thought to whether your revision environment is free from interruptions. You might be surprised at how much of your revision time is wasted as a result of distractions and interruptions.

Try carrying out a time audit of a two-hour revision period (or ordinary study period if you prefer) to see how many of those 120 minutes you spend working. Find a stopwatch or use the timer on your mobile phone and use it to time your revision/study period. Every time you stop working for any reason, make a note of the time and the reason that you stopped working. You should note the time that you start work again. At the end of the session, make a guess at how much time you spent doing things other than revising and then add up your 'minutes taken' column to see if your guess was accurate.

You will find a downloadable version of the form below on the Companion Website. One completed form is reproduced here along with a summary of the findings from one group of students who completed the time audit.

Start time	Stop time	Why did you stop?	Minutes taken
2.30pm	2.34pm	Went to get some notes from my bag.	2 minutes
2.36pm	2.38pm	Got a text. Sent a reply.	1 minute
2.39pm	2.44pm	Don't know. My mind just wandered.	3 minutes
2.47pm	2.58pm	Went to make coffee.	5 minutes
3.03pm	3.10pm	Got a text. Sent a reply.	1 minute
3.11pm	3.15pm	Checked email.	7 minutes
3.22pm	3.26pm	Got up for a bit of a stretch.	1 minute
3.27pm	3.33pm	Got a text. Sent a reply.	1 minute
3.34pm	3.50pm	Phone call.	4 minutes
3.54pm	4.15pm	Went to make coffee.	3 minutes
4.18pm	4.25pm	Got a text. Sent a reply.	1 minute
4.26pm	4.30pm	Checked email.	3 minutes
		Time spent on distractions	**32 minutes**

The student who completed this time audit had estimated that he only spent four minutes of the two-hour period doing things other than his revision. His reaction to the discovery that he had actually spent 32 minutes doing various other things was one of surprise:

I can't believe I spent that much time fiddling about. I actually thought that I'd worked solidly all the two hours. My guess for time wasted was four minutes so I'm really shocked that it was more than half an hour. The thing is that you don't feel like you're wasting time when you're doing these things. I just answer texts without knowing I'm doing it and I honestly thought that it took me less than a minute to make a cup of coffee. Checking my email was a bit unnecessary; I can't believe I did it at all, let alone doing it twice. I'm going to turn my phone and computer right off next time I revise.

Tom

The time audit can be a great way to identify poor working practices that interrupt revision as well as being a real eye-opener in terms of how much revision time is spent on things that are not revision; this is something that comes as a surprise to most students who complete the time audit. Taking one revision group of 14 students who carried out a time audit as an example:

- All of the students under-estimated how much time they had wasted. In six cases, the estimate of time spent on distractions was inaccurate by more than 25 minutes.

- Only three students spent more than one-and-a-half hours of the two-hour session on revision. Three students spent less than 30 minutes revising, thus using only a quarter of their revision time productively. The average time spent on revision was 75 minutes (just over half of the duration of the session).

- The biggest time-wasting activities across all students in the group were checking emails, sending texts and making telephone calls.

Planning your revision

Does this experience sound familiar?

I don't plan my revision. I just start. I pick a subject, grab my notes and get started. I don't know why I do it like that because I always end up spending too much time on some subjects and not enough on others so I feel a bit panicky about some of the exams.

Tom

Many students report that, like Tom, they 'just start' revision without any clear plan other than to get as much revision done as possible before the exams start. At the start of the revision period, there can be a sense that there is plenty of time before the exams start which leads to a leisurely approach to revision and a last-minute panic when the first exam is looming and there is a realisation that there is still much material to cover. Students who revise without a plan also tend to focus too much on the first exam and rely on the days between exams for revision of the other subjects.

In order to avoid these problems, you should take a little time to organise your revision and create a revision timetable that will ensure that you are working steadily and that all subjects are covered in equal depth.

In order to do this, you need to consider the questions shown in Figure 2.1.

Figure 2.1 Organising your revision: key questions

> **How much time is available?**
> Count the number of days from the start of the revision period to the date of the first exam, making sure that you take out an appropriate number of rest days.

> **What pattern of work suits you?**
> Do you work more effectively in the morning or later in the day?
> Do you work in short bursts or can you concentrate for four-hour stretches?

> **What topics should you revise?**
> This covers the number of topics that you should try to cover and the selection of topics for revision.

Calculate the time available

Do you know how long it is before your first exam? This is not the same thing as knowing what the date of the first exam is and it requires a more specific answer than 'about four weeks'. It is only when you know the exact amount of time available for revision that you can start to organise your work within it.

- **Pick a starting day for your revision.** Count the number of days until the first exam to calculate the number of days available for revision. It is a good idea to work on the assumption that the bulk of your revision will be complete by the time of the first exam so that you are not relying on the days in between the exams. Of course, these days can be used for revision and it would always be advisable to use them to ensure that topics are fresh in your mind, but try to avoid counting on them as a time to start revision of new topics.

■ **Decide how many of the available days will be used for revision.** It would be easy to respond 'all of them', but it is advisable to have rest days to ensure that you do not overwork during the revision period. If you feel anxious at the thought of taking a whole day off then give yourself some half days free to ensure that you get a break from revision.

■ **Think about how many hours you will want to work each day.** Again, try not to be unrealistic and set yourself too heavy a workload. An eight-hour day is reasonable and should not be too taxing but anything more than that could leave you over-tired and, in any case, you might find that your effectiveness for study is eroded once you work for too great a time period.

Once you can answer these questions, you will know the total number of revision hours available to you. You can then think about how to slot these into your timetable based upon your preferred pattern of work.

Select a pattern of work

Try to make everything that you do the consequence of conscious choice. In other words, instead of starting work every day at 9am, taking an hour for lunch at 1pm and working through to 6pm just because that is what you always do, take some time to consider whether there may be a different way to structure your day that will make your revision more effective.

Everybody has their own preferences when it comes to work patterns. Some people like to make an early start whilst others find it difficult to concentrate before lunchtime. Some students can work for many hours at a stretch whilst others find that they cannot concentrate if they work for more than one hour without a break.

Think about these two factors and devise a working pattern that suits you by considering these two questions:

■ **When do you feel most alert and productive?** Are you a morning person or do you prefer to start late and work late? If you struggle to make it to a lecture for 9am then it may be that you need to tailor your revision timetable so that you can start mid-morning. Some people find that their concentration is affected by factors such as food and exercise. Do you feel sluggish after lunch but find that you perk up if you go for a walk for half an hour? Some people cannot concentrate if they are hungry. These are all factors to take into account when planning your working day.

■ **How long can you concentrate on work without a break?** Think about the number of hours that you plan to work each day and then divide this into smaller revision sessions based upon the length of time that you can maintain concentration. For example, some people would feel happy with two four-hour periods of study in one day interrupted by a one-hour break whereas others would rather work for one hour at a time with a ten-minute break and half an hour for lunch. There is no right or wrong approach, so think about your preferences and break up your day into segments. There is no need for a uniform approach; perhaps you can work for four hours in the morning and then, after lunch, work in shorter one-hour bursts.

If you are unsure about what sort of work pattern suits you best, experiment with different approaches and see which one feels the most productive. Do not feel that you have to stick to the pattern every day; it can be refreshing to vary your working pattern and this can also be a way to incorporate rest periods into your revision plans.

Choose revision topics

There are two factors that are relevant to the selection of revision topics. Firstly, how many topics should you aim to cover in your revision? If you revise too many topics, there is a possibility that you will struggle to master all the material in sufficient depth within the timeframe of the revision period. However, if you cover too few topics, there is a very real risk that you will not know enough to tackle the required number of questions on the exam paper. The second issue to consider is which of the topics that were covered in a particular subject should be selected for revision.

How many topics to revise?

The question 'how many topics should I revise?' is one that is commonly asked of lecturers. Many lecturers will offer responses that seem unhelpful or unrealistic such as 'as many of the topics as you can manage' or 'all of the syllabus'. However, the logic behind this advice is sound as the more topics you revise, the more questions you should be able to tackle in the exam.

For many students, the aim is to revise as few topics as possible. This is not a matter of laziness or a disinterest in the subject matter, but a practical decision based upon the volume of work involved in mastering and remembering each topic. This is not unreasonable but it is essential that you remember that reducing the number of topics covered to the bare minimum (in other words, the number of questions that need to be answered) is a dangerous strategy that can leave students unprepared for the exam.

STUDENT EXPERIENCE

In all our exams we have to answer four questions from a choice of eight so, in my first year, I revised four topics for each exam. In the first exam, I was fine because I could answer three questions easily and remembered something from a tutorial for the last question, but the next exam was horrible. I read the questions and realised I could

▶

only answer one of them. I did try four questions but I didn't know anything about them and I knew I'd have to resit. I tried to cram for the last two exams but I didn't have much time and ended up with quite poor results. In my second year, there was no way I was going to make the same mistake again so I revised between eight and ten topics for each exam. I felt much better prepared and I didn't have any difficulty in answering four questions on every exam paper. In fact, in European law, I could actually have answered every question on the paper. I felt much more confident going into the exams knowing that I knew more topics and my results were much better.

Archana

Limiting your revision to the same number of topics as there are questions to be answered leaves you vulnerable to the following situations:

- If one or more of your topics do not come up on the paper, you will not be able to answer enough questions.

- If one of your topics is combined with another topic that you did not revise, you will have no choice other than to answer that question, even though you know that you cannot deal with all of the issues that it raises.

- If one of your topics comes up in a form that you did not anticipate (if you have revised for a problem question but the topic is examined as an essay question) or if you do not understand what the question means, you will have to struggle on with it.

In essence, these are all manifestations of the same problem: lack of choice. If you have revised four topics for an exam where you have to answer four questions, you have made your success in the exam utterly reliant on those topics coming up on the paper in a form that you can tackle.

Try to avoid this situation by increasing the number of topics that you revise. Base your decision on the number of topics that were covered in each module and aim to revise at least half that number if you can manage it in the time available. Alternatively, you could make a calculation on the basis of the number of questions plus two as that should provide you with at least a little choice in the exam.

Which topics to revise?

It would be very difficult to give advice on which topics to revise as there are subject specific factors to take into account as well as the personal preferences that each student will have about the difficulty or interest of each topic. The following is a list of factors to consider as they could affect topic choice:

- **How much time was spent on the topic in lectures?** Look at the way that the subject is divided into topics on the course syllabus and think about how much time was given to each topic in lectures. For example, it is likely that a great deal more lecture time was devoted to negligence than was given to trespass to the person in tort. This should give you an idea of how significant each topic is within the module so it would be sensible to prioritise accordingly when making your selection.

- **What topics did you find enjoyable and easy to understand?** Try to play to your strengths wherever possible. It is always easier to remember material that you find of interest so try to prioritise topics that you found enjoyable. If you really disliked a particular topic, did not understand it or have incomplete notes if you missed periods of study due to illness then it may be that the revision period is not the time to try to master them. Remember that the purpose of revision is to revisit material that you already understand, not to learn it for the first time.

- **Do you have any insight into which topics will be examined?** Lecturers will sometimes advise students that particular topics will or will not appear on the exam paper. For example, you may be told that the coursework topic will not be re-examined or a lecturer may announce the topic of the compulsory question if one is featured in the exam. Be careful, though, with anything other than direct information as unfounded rumours often circulate about exam topics and this can be very distracting.

- **Use past papers for guidance.** You can get a good idea of how topics are examined and how they combine with other topics by looking at past papers. Remember, though, that past papers can only give you insight into how topics have appeared in the past and should not be used as the basis for predictions about what will feature in future exams. You will find more discussion of the value of past papers in revision in Chapter 6.

 Try this

Test your topic selection

Taking into account the advice given in this section of the book, make a decision about how many topics you will revise for one of your modules and then make a list of the topics that you would select for revision.

Using the resources available at your university, find a past paper from the previous year and analyse it to see whether you would have been able to answer the required number of questions on the basis of the topics that you had planned to revise. Repeat this with more than one past paper to allow for variation in the topics covered.

This should give you some insight into whether or not you have chosen enough topics and selected a good range of topics.

Create a revision timetable

The final stage of revision planning is the construction of a revision timetable. It is important to do this as it gives you a visual reminder of your planned schedule of work so that you can keep an eye on your progress. It is also useful to be able to start each revision session with a clear idea of what it is that you are going to cover and what you plan to achieve.

Armed with knowledge of the time available, your preferred patterns of study and your revision topics, construct a timetable that maps out your activities for each day. Start by allocating each day a topic, making a decision about whether you want to cluster all your revision of a particular subject together (as you see in Figure 2.2) or if you want to alternate subjects (perhaps you could revise offer and acceptance one day followed by sexual offences and then judicial review).

The next step is to formulate a plan of each day (Figure 2.3). This should have periods of revision in which you try to commit the topic to memory interspersed with test periods to determine whether or not the material is sticking in your mind. You will find some suggestions of the sorts of activities that you could incorporate into your revision in Chapter 3.

In Figure 2.3, you will see that the plan is divided into periods of revision in which material is reviewed and committed to memory that are interspersed with tests to determine whether the material can be recalled. There are also plenty of rest breaks. Note that there are numerous other ways in which a day of revision could be structured; this is just one example.

Remember that a revision timetable is not set in stone. It exists to help you to use your revision time effectively so that you are prepared for all your exams. If you find that your planned approach is not working then you should think about what has gone wrong and make changes to your timetable. For example, you may find that one day of revision for each topic is just not enough or that the working pattern that you thought would work leaves you exhausted by mid-afternoon in which case you can reconstruct your timetable to take account of these problems.

Similarly, if you have formulated a timetable based upon the suggestions in this chapter and you find that it works well for you, do not be alarmed if you find that other students are approaching their revision in a very different way. Remember that study patterns, topic preferences and revision activities are highly individual matters so what works for one student will not work for another.

EXAM TIP

Do not take too long to plan your revision. Remember that time is in limited supply before the exams and you need to spend this time working on your revision, not creating your revision timetable. Allocate one morning to the task of getting organised and then get on with the all-important task of revising.

Figure 2.2 Monthly revision timetable

Monday	Tuesday	Wednesday	Thursday	Friday	Saturday	Sunday
1	**2**	**3**	**4**	**5**	**6**	**7**
Sexual offences	Sexual offences Non-fatals	Non-fatals	Duress Self-defence	Homicide	Homicide Criminal damage	Rest
8	**9**	**10**	**11**	**12**	**13**	**14**
Judicial review	Judicial review	Separation of powers	Convention rights	Rule of Law Parl Sov	Judicial review	Rest
15	**16**	**17**	**18**	**19**	**20**	**21**
Offer and acceptance	Mistake Misrep	UCTA	UCTA	Terms Conditions Warranties	Remedies	Rest
22	**23**	**24**	**25**	**26**	**27**	**28**
Statutory interpretation	Statutory interpretation	Precedent	Appeals	Court systems	Jury system	Rest

Figure 2.3 Daily revision timetable

Monday 1st		Tuesday 2nd	
10–11.30	Sexual offences revision	10–11.30	Sexual offences practice question
11.30–11.45	Break	11.30–11.45	Break
11.45–12.30	Sexual offences test	11.45–12.30	Review sexual offences question
12.30–1	Check test and correct errors	12.30–1	Start non-fatal offences revision
1–1.30	Lunch	1–1.30	Lunch
1.30–2.15	Sexual offences practice question	1.30–2.15	Non-fatal offences revision
2.15–2.30	Break	2.15–2.30	Break
2.30–3.30	Check question against notes	2.30–3.30	Non-fatal offences test
3.30–4.15	Revisit sexual offences problem areas	3.30–4.15	Check test and correct errors
4.15–7.30	Break	4.15–7.30	Break
7.30–8.30	Review sexual offences notes	7.30–8.30	Review non-fatal offences notes

www.pearsoned.co.uk/lawexpress

■ To find out more ...

Visit the Companion Website where you will find some resources to help you with your revision planning. You will find more information on how to carry out a time audit with some suggestions for eliminating your worst time-wasting habits. There is also a downloadable revision calendar that you can download and use to create a personalised revision timetable.

NOTES

NOTES

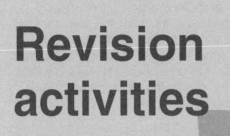

Revision
activities

Revision checklist

Topics covered in this chapter:

- [ ] Taking an effective approach to revision
- [ ] Understanding, memorising and using the law
- [ ] Making notes and other methods of recording information
- [ ] Revising for essays and problem questions
- [ ] Activities to test your memory
- [ ] Writing practice answers

■ Introduction

The aim of revision is to ensure that you are able to perform well in the exam and achieve good marks. In order to perform well in the exam, you need to have a solid understanding of the law, an ability to remember sufficient law to answer the required number of questions and the skills to use the law effectively to create focused responses to the essay and problem questions on the exam paper. This means that your revision should comprise a mix of activities focused on these three areas of understanding, memorisation and deployment of the law. This chapter will outline a range of activities relating to each of these three core areas and explain how they will help you to prepare for the exam. Before doing this, the chapter will start by highlighting some other factors that contribute to the effectiveness of revision.

■ Effective revision

STUDENT EXPERIENCE

When it's time to start, I tend to just pick up a textbook, read the chapter that seems most appealing and make notes on it. I know that this is a bit aimless and my marks are never as good as I'd like so it probably isn't the best use of my revision time but it's what I've always done and, to be honest, I can't ever really think of anything else to do.

Tom

You can measure the effectiveness of your revision strategy by the success or otherwise of your exam marks. If, like Tom, your marks are never as high as you would like, then it would be sensible to make changes to the way that you revise for the exams. There is a famous quote that says 'if you always do what you've always done, you'll always get what you've always got' so if you do not want to continue getting the same level of marks for your exams then you should not stick to the same methods of revision that have produced these results so far. Make this the year that you try some different activities as part of your revision as this should lead to an improvement in the marks that you receive.

Active and varied revision

Revision should be both active and varied. Active revision involves doing something with the material that you are trying to learn rather than just reading and re-writing your notes. This approach of reading and re-writing is commonly used by students but is not particularly beneficial because it does not do enough to target any of the three skills of understanding, memorising and using the law that are at the heart of effective revision. It is essential that your revision targets all three skills, as the absence of any one will impact on the success of your answers in the exam.

- **Lack of understanding.** If you do not understand the law, you will have to commit it to memory without any idea of what it means or how it operates. You will be able to reproduce chunks of memorised law in the exam, but your lack of understanding will significantly limit your ability to use the law to produce answers.

- **Failure of memory.** If you understand the law but cannot remember it, then you will not be able to reproduce what you know in the exam and your answers will have significant gaps and lack a sound legal basis.

- **Ineffective use of the law.** Do not expect to be rewarded for remembering the law: examiners want to see if you can use it to create analytical essays and well-argued answers to problem questions.

It is the need to strengthen all three skills that gives rise to the importance of engaging in a range of revision activities to ensure that each of the skills is targeted. Unfortunately, students tend to prioritise memorisation during the revision period, assuming that understanding is measured by the volume of accurate law reproduced in the exam booklet and overlooking the need to use the law entirely.

 Lecturer viewpoint

Exams should be a test of knowledge, not of memory. It is always easy to spot answers that are based upon memorised chunks of law and they attract very little credit because it is not possible for me to assess whether the student actually understands what they have written.

Maximise the efficacy of your revision by combining activities that promote understanding, aid memory and recall and strengthen your ability to use the law effectively. Not only should this enable you to produce answers in the exam that are more successful, as they demonstrate all three core skills, but the variety will also make the revision process more enjoyable and engaging.

Getting started

It is important that you make a start on your revision as soon as possible. It is not even necessary to wait until teaching has finished before you start to revise: there are activities that can be done from the beginning of the module that will give you a running start once the revision period arrives.

Try this

Make an early start

Make revision aids such as flashcards and quizzes on each topic as it is taught when it is fresh in your mind. You will then have a good stock of materials to use in your revision.

Unfortunately, some students find the idea of revision so daunting or are so unsure as to how to go about revising that they find excuses to put off getting started. The effectiveness of your revision will be reduced if you put off starting it for so long that you do not have enough time remaining to cover a sufficient number of topics in an appropriate level of detail.

STUDENT EXPERIENCE

I spend so much time planning my revision so that I can feel like I'm working towards my exams, but I do know secretly that I'm putting off actually starting my revision. I've got a colour-coded revision timetable, my notes and books are in neat piles and I've even got a row of sharpened pencils but I'm still trying to find an excuse not to start actually revising.

Emily

This is a very common experience. Students know that they need to revise – indeed, they are often consumed with a sense of urgency about getting their revision underway – but they do not have a clear idea of what it is that they need to do. This can lead students to engage in displacement activities such as excessive planning as a means of deferring the start of their revision. Obviously, this is not a good strategy because it further reduces the already limited time available for revision.

EXAM TIP

It is psychologically important to get your revision off to a good start. Set a first task for yourself which is realistic and which has a visible outcome so that you feel that you have achieved something positive as a result of your first revision session. This could be consolidating your notes into a series of key points and cases, producing a mind map of a particular topic or creating a glossary of key terms to commit to memory. It is important that you reach the end of your first session with a sense of satisfaction and a positive feeling about your revision.

■ Revision notes

A good set of revision notes is an essential component of successful revision. This statement may seem to contradict the point made earlier in this chapter about the limited effectiveness of reading and re-writing revision notes. However, there is no conflict: revision notes are a valuable *part* of revision, but your revision should not consist *only* of reading and re-writing these notes in the hope that they will stick in your memory. In the sections that follow, you will find guidance that will help you to produce effective revision notes and use them in a way that strengthens your understanding of the law and your ability to retrieve information from your memory when it is needed in the exam room.

Creating revision notes

It is a good idea to create a fresh set of notes from scratch that are tailored to your revision. Many students prefer not to do this, feeling that it takes up too much time, and instead revise from their lecture notes. This is not a good idea. One of the aims of the revision process is to strengthen understanding and this is not achieved by relying on half-remembered notes taken months ago in a lecture, particularly if you never really got to grips with the topic at the time. Moreover, lecture notes are designed to give you an outline of a topic that you supplement with your own private study, so it is unlikely that all the information that you need to prepare for the exam is to be found in your lecture notes.

 Lecturer viewpoint

Some students seem to think that the purpose of the exam is to test whether they can memorise my lecture notes and write them out in the exam. Some answers consist of nothing except the same points that I made in the lecture in exactly the same order that I made them, which I find very annoying.

Make sure that your revision notes prepare you to produce answers that demonstrate your own independent study by using your lecture notes in conjunction with other sources (see Figure 3.1) to produce a comprehensive set of notes that contains all the points that you would like to remember about a particular topic.

The word 'revision' comes from the Latin *revisere* meaning 'to look at again' which conveys the idea that revision involves revisiting knowledge that has already been acquired. Whilst this implies that the bulk of your knowledge of the law should already be in place, it does not mean that you cannot add to your understanding of a topic during the revision period. In fact, one of your key objectives in the revision period should be to consolidate

Figure 3.1 Sources of revision notes

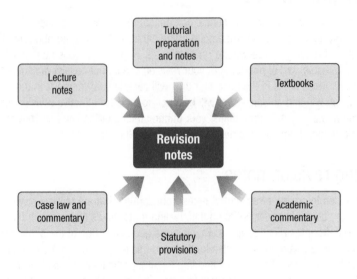

your knowledge and this includes identifying and plugging any gaps in your knowledge. Remember, though, that learning a new topic that you did not previously understand involves a lot more work than dealing with a few gaps in your knowledge of a topic that you have, by and large, already grasped. Any attempt to tackle a wholly unfamiliar topic within the revision period should be approached with caution.

EXAM TIP

Be realistic about what you can achieve in the revision period. It might be better to accept that you are never going to understand a particular topic, even if it is almost certain to be on the exam paper, and focus your attention on other areas of law where your understanding is stronger. It will take you longer to learn a new topic from scratch than it will to strengthen your knowledge of law that you already understand.

Reading, writing and condensing notes

The first objective of note-making during the revision period is to create a comprehensive set of notes that reflects the depth of your understanding of a topic and which notes all the key points and cases that you would like to be able to call to mind in the exam. The second objective is to shift most of the detail from the page into your brain so that it can be recalled when prompted by one of a series of key words or phrases. In other words, you should aim to make your notes progressively more condensed until they consist only of a skeleton composed of these key words and phrases which will then trigger your memory of the full body of knowledge that lies behind them.

Example: Condensed notes

You should aim to reduce the size of your notes on each topic as your revision progresses; as you remember more, you should write less. This example shows how the main statutory provisions and cases in theft that originally covered several pages can be reduced to a list of points and key cases.

Notes on the elements of theft in criminal law

Theft defined in section 1 Theft Act 1968.

Section 2 – **dishonesty** (negative definition, subjective)

> (a) belief that he has right in law to property
> (b) belief in owner's consent
> (c) belief owner cannot be found

> *Ghosh* test: ordinary standards of reasonable and honest people.

Section 3 – **appropriation**: assumption of the rights of the owner

> *Lawrence* – taxi driver, can happen with consent
> *Morris* – price labels, adverse interference and any of the rights
> *Gomez* – electrical shop, not adverse interference
> *Hinks* – appropriation and gifts

Section 4 – **property**: all things, money, things in action.

> Excluded by *Oxford* v. *Moss*: confidential information
> Excluded by statute: land, growing things, animals

Section 5 – **belonging to another**

> (1) possession and control (*Turner No 2* – theft of own car)
> (3) duty to use in particular way (*Wain* – charity money, *Hall* – travel agent)
> (4) got by mistake (*Shadrokh-Cigari* – £286,000 instead of £286)

Section 6 – **intention to permanently deprive**

> (1) borrowing may be equivalent to taking

> *Lloyd* – cinema films, extinguish value and goodness

The other advantage of this approach is that you should be able to visualise the layout of the notes on the page and that should help you to recall their content in the exam.

Condensing notes is a useful activity as it bridges the gap between understanding and memory by increasing the volume of knowledge stored in the brain and reducing the pressure on your memory by ensuring that this knowledge can be triggered by a few key words and phrases.

By contrast, simply reading and copying out notes in the hope that this fixes them in your brain is not a good use of your time as it will not enhance your ability to understand and remember the law. In fact, reading notes and copying them out repeatedly will actually give you a false sense that the content has been stored in your memory: you will remember having encountered it before and assume, quite wrongly, that this means that you will remember it in the exam.

STUDENT EXPERIENCE

I used to read my notes through and write them out a few times. After that, it was all so familiar that I'd think that I'd got it so I'd move on to something else. In the exam, when I needed to remember something about a topic, I found that I could remember reading it but I couldn't remember what it said. Needless to say, my results were not good that year.

Matt

There is a world of difference between the ability to remember that you have read your notes before when they are in front of you and the ability to recall them in the exam when there is nothing there to trigger your memory. Do not make the mistake of confusing the two things and make sure that you take an active approach that involves doing something with your material, rather than just reading it or writing it out, as this will increase the chances of it sticking in your brain.

Mind maps and flow charts

You do not have to make linear notes in order to capture your understanding of the law. Some students prefer to create mind maps or flow charts that illustrate the connection between different pieces of information. You will find some examples of these methods in Chapter 5.

There are two ways in which the creation of mind maps and flow charts contributes to your revision. Firstly, the process of selecting points to include and organising them in a systematic way tests your understanding of the topic and, secondly, the creation of a visual structure in which key words and phrases appear can really aid memory.

EXAM TIP

Once you have finalised the design of your mind map or flow chart, draw up or print (depending upon whether you produced it by hand or on a computer) a number of blank versions. Test your ability to fill the detail into the blank spaces frequently to fix the content in your memory. Once you are confident in doing this, practise producing the whole diagram from memory.

Audio recordings

You can also make an audio recording of your revision notes. This can be particularly useful to add variety to your revision as it targets your brain via the ears instead of the eyes. This method also enables you to revise without having to take notes with you, so some people like to listen to a recording at the gym or whilst out walking. If you are considering making some revision recordings, you might like to bear in mind the following tips to maximise their usefulness:

- **Plan your content.** Do not just record yourself reading your notes or a textbook. Put time and effort into selecting relevant material and structuring your content so that it provides you with a self-contained discussion of a particular topic. Remember, this process will strengthen your understanding, so it is a valuable aspect of your revision in its own right.

- **Signpost your recording.** It is important that your recording is easy to follow, so ensure that you include plenty of signposting: phrases such as 'there are three points to remember' and 'five different cases deal with this issue' will help you to slot the information together and give you a clearer grasp of the topic. You should also find that signposting helps you to remember the structure as well as the content of your recording which will be useful when you need to recall the information in the exam.

- **Keep it short.** There is a limit to how much information your brain can process at any one time without a break, so do not overwhelm it with information. Moreover, listening to yourself rambling on about the law for hours is not engaging so your brain may well 'tune out' and start thinking about something more interesting. A short and focused recording of no more than 20 minutes is far more engaging for your brain as it is more likely that you will listen and digest the information.

- **Repetition aids recollection.** Bear in mind that the purpose of your recording is to enable you to remember, so be sure to repeat key information to help it stick in your memory. It would also be useful to conclude your recording with a summary of its key points or cases.

- **Include memory tests.** Make your recording more interactive by asking yourself questions and leaving spaces for an answer. Make sure that you then provide the answer to maximise the effectiveness of the exercise.

You will find an example of a short revision recording on the Companion Website along with an annotated transcript that will help you to understand how it was put together in a way that took into account these points.

Tailored notes

Do you tailor your revision towards either an essay or a problem question? Most students revise a topic without ever giving any consideration to what sort of question they will encounter in the exam.

Lecturer viewpoint

A student was discussing his problems with understanding the incorporation of contract terms with me. I asked if he was preparing for an essay or a problem and he said 'no, it's for the exams' as this was a wholly different species of assessment. I spent some time with him but he didn't seem to understand that he needed to have different material at his fingertips to do well in an essay than he would to tackle a problem question on the same subject matter.

It is often the case that students fail to tailor their revision because they want to be able to write an essay or answer a problem question on the topic. This is perfectly understandable, but it is important to appreciate the different requirements of the two types of question and tailor your revision accordingly to ensure that you are prepared for a question of either type or, if you have a preference, that you select material to maximise the effectiveness of your revision for your chosen type of question.

Revising for an essay

An essay will ask you a specific question about a particular topic. You might be able to predict what topics will appear on the exam paper with a fair degree of confidence, but it is very unlikely that you will be able to anticipate what question will be asked about that topic. In other words, you may be able to work out what general area of law will be the focus of a question, but you will not know what particular line of discussion will be required about that topic.

Figure 3.2 Different lines of discussion around core content

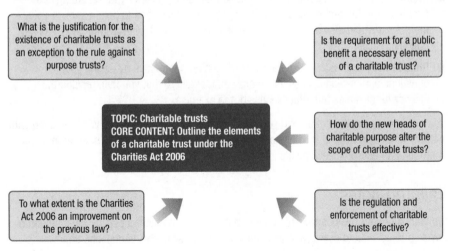

Therefore, in order to be effective, your revision for an essay question should have at its core the main elements of the topic that will be useful irrespective of what question is asked. This corresponds with the descriptive foundation of your essay (see Chapter 8 for guidance on achieving a balance between analysis and description in the exam). In addition to this, you will need to anticipate what questions could be asked about the topic and then ensure that your revision covers material that enables you to engage in an appropriate discussion (see Figure 3.2).

EXAM TIP

Spend some time thinking about the sorts of question that could be asked about a topic. Has anything about the area of law changed recently? Is there new legislation or has a case been decided that expands or restricts the scope of the law? Are there any proposals for reform? Think about the focus of discussion in tutorials and whether your attention was pointed towards any particular issues in lectures. Look for recent journal articles to see what sorts of discussion are taking place about the topic. These sources may give you some insight into the sorts of questions that could be asked about the topic, but it is also worth remembering that a great many essay questions simply ask 'is the law effective?' in a variety of different wording.

Once you have identified some potential questions that could be asked about a topic, try grouping together the points from your notes that would answer these questions. As a rough rule of thumb, try to ensure that you could make three separate arguments about any particular question. You might find that journal articles are an especially useful source of inspiration that will help you to identify points to support your discussion.

Revising for a problem question

Problem questions are more likely to combine different topics together in a single question, so your revision should cover as much of the syllabus as possible to reflect this. To answer a problem question to a high standard requires breadth of knowledge about the current law in operation. In other words, unlike an essay, you do not need to know how the law used to be, how it might be in the future or what is wrong with it: you just need to be able to state the current law and apply it to the facts (see Chapter 9 for more guidance on this).

However, the ability to apply the law requires a comprehensive knowledge of case law as it is by using cases that you can demonstrate in your answer how the law is likely to apply. This means that you need to know not only the leading cases that set out the core principles of the law but also a range of cases that demonstrate how that principle applies in a variety of different factual situations.

EXAM TIP

Try not to overwhelm your brain with details of case law. Adopt a systematic approach to extracting the relevant information from a case and try to capture this concisely.

Case name   *Fisher* v. *Bell*

Facts   Flick knife was displayed in a shop window with a price label attached.

Principle   Offers must be capable of immediate acceptance.

Purpose   Use this to demonstrate an invitation to treat.

You may find case summaries in revision guides useful in helping you to distil the important information from a case. Here is an example of the key case feature from the *Law Express* series which highlights the legal principles that arise from the case in question:

KEY CASE

Young **v.** *Bristol Aeroplane Co. Ltd* **[1944] KB 718**

Concerning: Court of Appeal bound by its own decisions

Legal principle

The Court of Appeal held that it is normally bound by its previous decisions, subject to three exceptions:

- **Where its own previous decisions conflict.** This may arise if the court in the later case was unaware of the decision of the earlier case; for instance, if the earlier case was very recent or unreported, or the second case might have distinguished the first, or one of the cases had been decided *per incuriam* (see below). In such situations, the Court of Appeal can choose which of its previous decisions to follow and which to reject. Whilst this has obvious implications for the future precedent value of the decision which is not followed, its status is not technically affected by the fact that it has not been followed; it could still be adopted in subsequent cases.
- **Where its previous decision had been implicitly overruled by the House of Lords.** This occurs when a previous Court of Appeal decision is inconsistent with a later House of Lords decision. This could occur where a case has bypassed the Court of Appeal and gone straight to the House of Lords (by the 'leapfrog procedure' – see Chapter 7 on the appeals process).
- **Where its previous decision was made *per incuriam*.** A decision made *per incuriam* is one made 'through carelessness' or without due regard to the relevant law. It should not be confused with *per curiam* which is a part of a judgment upon which all the judges are agreed.

■ Testing your memory

The activities outlined in this chapter so far have concentrated on the production of a set of easily digestible notes that capture your understanding of the law and which can be learned and stored in your memory. The focus of this section is a series of activities that will be valuable in testing whether or not the relevant material has been committed to memory and can be retrieved on demand. Such activities are an essential aspect of revision as you need to know whether your attempts to commit the law to memory have been successful so that you can make changes if necessary. In addition to this, the ability to retrieve information from your memory will improve with practice: in essence, the more you practise remembering during the revision period, the more you will be able to remember in the exam.

You will find a further discussion of the way that memory works, along with some suggestions for more activities to strengthen your powers of recall, in Chapter 5.

Revision flashcards

Revision flashcards are small (and therefore very portable) cards that have a prompt written on the front and the response on the reverse. This prompt and response can take a number of forms as illustrated in Table 3.1.

Prompt	Response	Front	Back
Question	Answer	What is the test of dishonesty?	There are two questions: (1) was the conduct dishonesty according to the standards of a reasonable and honest person and (2) if so, was the defendant aware that his conduct was dishonest according to that standard.
Key term	Definition	Innominate term	A contract term which is neither a condition nor a warranty, but which may be treated as either one depending on the severity of the consequences of the breach.
Case name	Facts and principle	*ex parte Rose Theatre Group*	An interest group was formed to oppose plans to demolish the Rose Theatre. It was held that individuals who do not have standing to bring a claim for judicial review could not gain standing by gathering together in a group.

▶

Journal article	List of key points	Reece – *Modern Law Review* – loss of chance	Explains the meaning between 'determinism' and 'indeterminism' in loss of chance cases in tort.
			Deterministic = past uniquely determines future
			Indeterministic = random component involved

Table 3.1 Sample flashcards

Flashcards are particularly useful to test your ability to recall relatively straightforward pieces of factual knowledge. You can use them alone, reading the question and deciding on a response before turning the card over, or you can recruit other people to test your knowledge. As the flashcards contain the prompt and the expected response, you can be tested by people who have no legal knowledge, which should expand your group of potential helpers.

The process of creating the flashcards will contribute to your revision as you will need a good knowledge of the topic in order to be able to identify suitable questions to ask and the correct answer to them. A further advantage of flashcards is that they can be prepared well in advance of the revision period.

STUDENT EXPERIENCE

I work with three friends and we all make five flashcards after each lecture. We do get a bit of overlap sometimes if more than one of us asks the same question but we still end up with a big pile of flashcards by the time teaching has finished.

Eloise

You will find examples of revision flashcards on the Companion Website of the *Law Express* revision guides at www.pearsoned.co.uk/lawexpress

Fill in the gap

Another useful method of testing your powers of recall is the 'fill in the gaps' exercise. As the name suggests, this involves creating an outline of a topic with some crucial information missing to see if you are able to remember and add the missing points. You can do this with your revision notes once you have condensed a topic down to its bare bones or you can create blank versions of mind maps and flow charts to test your ability to fill in the detail.

Example: Fill in the gaps

The template below is based upon the condensed notes on theft that you will find earlier in this chapter on page 41. As you will see, the template contains some information to act as a prompt but the aim is to reach a point where the notes can be reproduced without any such clues as to content.

Notes on the elements of theft in criminal law

Theft defined in section 1 Theft Act 1968.

Section 2 – **d**_____ (n_____ d_____, sub_____)

    (a)

    (b)

    (c)

    *G*_____ test: o_____ s_____ of r_____ and h_____ p_____

Section 3 – **a**_____ (a_____ of the r_____ of the o_____)

    L _____ facts:

    M _____ facts:

    G _____ facts:

    H _____ facts:

Quizzes

Quizzes are also a good way to test your memory. Create them in conjunction with your revision notes so that each key point has a corresponding question. This approach ensures that you will be able to test your knowledge of a topic as soon as you have finished your notes on it to see how much information you retained. You can try to improve your accuracy after a period of learning your notes and test how much you can remember a day or a week after revising the topic.

EXAM TIP

Make quizzes of varying levels of difficulty. For example, you might start with a quiz that asks general questions about a topic such as occupiers' liability and then take a more specific focus with a quiz that looks at a particular issue such as liability to trespassers and then finish with a far more testing quiz that asks ten questions about a specific case such as *Keown* v. *Coventry Healthcare Trust* that deals with the extent of liability to child trespassers.

This method of revision can be particularly effective if you are working with other students (see Chapter 4). This is because there can be a tendency only to ask questions on material that you have understood; if you have not grasped a particular point, it is very hard to ask a question about it and work out the answer. By swapping quizzes with other students, you are gaining an insight into the points about a topic that they felt were important as well as encountering questions that you might have omitted as a result of a lack of understanding. This can really help you to identify gaps in your knowledge that need to be addressed prior to the exam. Make the most of this collaborative exercise by working together after you have taken the quiz to clarify any areas of uncertainty.

How much do you know?

This is a very simple way to test your memory. After you have revised a topic, find a blank sheet of paper and write a key word, phrase or case name at the top. Give yourself a period of time – anything between one minute and half an hour depending on the complexity of the topic – to write as much as you can remember about it. There is no need to think about the order in which you make the points: just see how much you can get down on paper. It is a good idea to do this with a pen and paper rather than typing as this will help you get into practice for the exam.

At the end of your period of time, look to see if there are any differences between what you have written and your revision notes:

- **Did you leave out any key points?** This should draw your attention to the need to focus on the omitted material to ensure it is fixed more firmly in your brain.

- **Did you remember more detail than your notes?** This is a good sign as it should reassure you that you have taken in the knowledge behind the notes. The ability to access a store of knowledge by memorising key words is one of the objectives of revision.

You can repeat this exercise at different points of your revision to test the effectiveness of your retention and recall.

> **EXAM TIP**
>
> This technique can be really useful if you find that you are stuck in the exam and cannot remember anything about a particular topic. Take a sheet of rough paper or a fresh page at the back of your exam booklet and write the word or phrase at the top of the page and write down everything that comes to mind. You will be surprised how one idea leads to another. Do make sure that you only select the really relevant points to include in your answer, though.

Give a lecture

Collect together a small group of students and offer to give a lecture on a particular topic (you might want to extract some sort of promise of assistance in return from them). How does this test your memory? Well, as you are doubtless aware from your own experiences, it is not very engaging for an audience to listen to a lecturer read from their notes so you will want to deliver your lecture without notes. You should prepare a plan of your lecture to help you remember what points you want to make, and in what order, but otherwise you should be working from your memory.

 Try this

Create a PowerPoint presentation

Many universities will allow students to use seminar rooms and lecture theatres that have PowerPoint facilities. Book one of these rooms and deliver your lecture with the assistance of PowerPoint slides to remind you of the structure of your lecture.

The value of this exercise is that it requires a combination of understanding and memory. It is not enough to list a series of remembered points: a lecture will only make sense if you have a firm understanding of the concepts that you are explaining, as the ability to explain the law in your own words is a true measure of your knowledge. It is also a test of your ability to communicate your understanding of the law with clarity – albeit orally rather than in writing – which is essential if you want to perform well in the exams. If you really want to make the most of this activity, encourage your audience to ask questions and see how well you can respond.

■ Writing practice answers

In most other areas of life, you practise something if you want to be good at it. For some reason, students seem to think that this does not apply to exams, assuming that they will be able to produce good quality answers in exam conditions despite not having done this, if at all, since the last exam period. Do not make the mistake of thinking that your experience of writing essays and answering problem questions for coursework obviates the need to practise producing answers to exam questions. Coursework and exams differ in a number of significant ways:

- **Time constraints.** You have approximately 45 minutes (depending on the length of the exam and the number of questions to be answered) to read the question, work out what it wants, comb your memory for relevant information and plan, write and check your answer.
- **No sources.** You cannot check with other students to make sure you have understood the question or to query what points to include. You cannot look the law up in a textbook or use any sources to get inspiration for your arguments.

■ **Write by hand.** You have to produce handwritten answers that can be read by the examiner. You cannot move paragraphs around to change the line of argument or insert points that you have forgotten as you could if you were producing coursework on a computer and you have no spelling and grammar checker to help you with accuracy.

In light of these points, it is not reasonable to assume that producing three or four pieces of coursework during the academic year will prepare you to produce three or four answers in a three-hour exam. Therefore, it would be sensible to incorporate writing practice answers into your revision.

STUDENT EXPERIENCE

I didn't see the point of writing practice answers from past papers, but one of my friends does it a lot and gets much better exam results than me so I thought I'd try it. It was a real eye-opener. I had four questions from past papers on a topic that I thought I'd actually revised really well, but I couldn't actually answer any of them. So I made a lot of changes to the way that I revised, tried again and did much better. It made an enormous difference to how well I was able to answer the questions in the exam and I got much better marks.

Lauren

Finding questions

It is likely that your university has a selection of past papers available that you will be able to use. These are usually stored online so make a point of finding out where they are, so that you can consult them during the revision period: even if you decide not to write practice answers, it is important that you know the sorts of questions that may be asked about a topic so that you can prepare effectively. If you are taking a module that is running for the first time, there will not be any past papers for you to consult so it would be worth asking the lecturer to produce a sample paper or at least some sample questions so that you can practise. You can also write practice answers to previous coursework questions and tutorial questions. Finally, some revision books, such as the *Law Express* series, contain sample exam questions and offer guidance on how they should be tackled that you might find useful.

Producing answers

The aim of this activity is to improve your ability to produce good answers in the exam. As such, you should ensure that your answers are produced in conditions that simulate – so far as possible – those that you will encounter in the exam. You should produce a handwritten answer without using your notes within the same time constraints that will exist in the exam.

This is one of the most useful activities that you can do during the revision period as it will help you to determine whether you know enough about a topic and whether you can produce

Lecturer viewpoint

I do offer to mark practice answers from my students, but only if they are proper practice answers writing by hand without notes within 40 minutes. There is no point in me giving feedback on answers that don't do this as it won't actually be useful to them.

your answers in the timeframe available in the exam. You can then make adjustments to what you are doing to overcome any problems that you encounter: for example, plugging gaps in your knowledge. You should find that you are able to manage your time more effectively in the exam as you will develop a real feel for how much you can write in 45 minutes.

Getting feedback

One of the reasons that students often give for their disinclination to write practice answers is that it is not possible to get feedback on them. What they mean by this is that it is not always possible to find a lecturer who will mark and comment on practice answers. This may well be the case (if a lecturer has 100 students and they all produce a practice answer, that is a lot of marking), but you may be able to find a lecturer who is willing to do this so it is always worth asking. If you can find a lecturer who will take the time to talk you through your answers then you should take advantage of this as their guidance and suggestions could really make a difference to the quality of the answers that you produce in the exam.

In the absence of this, you could use other students as a source of feedback. This works most effectively if you all attempt the same question and then distribute your answers around the group. Not only will this give you the benefit of their comments on your answer, but you will get to see how they went about tackling the question, which might give you some ideas on how to improve your own work.

Finally, you should strive to develop the ability to assess your own work with a critical eye. Of course, it can be difficult to pick up on errors or confusion in your own answers because you can at least compare the practice answer to your notes to see if you forgot anything important. Even if you cannot get anyone else to comment on your answers, remember that part of the value of the exercise lies in honing your ability to produce complete answers without notes by hand within the time constraints of the exam.

STUDENT EXPERIENCE

I aim to answer three different practice questions on every topic I revise. I do the first one as soon as I've revised the topic to see if I've learned enough, the second one a week later to see what I've remembered and the third one on the day before the exam to make sure that I am ready.

Lauren

www.pearsoned.co.uk/lawexpress

■ To find out more …

Visit the Companion Website where you will find some more examples of the
activities outlined in this chapter. Use this to produce similar resources to use in
your own revision. If you produce something that you feel is particularly useful,
why not send it to us and we may be able to use it on the Companion Website as a
good example of an effective revision activity. You will find details of how to contact
the authors on the Companion Website.

NOTES

Working with others

4

Introduction

As you will have seen in the last chapter, one of the key ways in which you can make your revision more effective is by ensuring that it is *active* revision. Chapter 3 covered a range of activities that you can try to ensure that your personal revision is active. However, another way of making revision more interesting (and thus effective) is to work with others.

It is, however, true to say that working in a group does not necessarily suit everyone. Some students hate the prospect of studying with their peers. However, if your personality is such that you enjoy group discussions and want to learn from others (and the others in the group think in the same way) then working with others can be an excellent way of strengthening your own exam performance. At the very least you should consider whether you might like to join – or form – a study group with other students.

Why work with others?

 Lecturer viewpoint

If a study group works well, then it can really help students to reinforce their learning and deepen their understanding of a subject. This depth of understanding leads on to better exam performance. But it's not for everyone. I have students that would rather jump off a bridge than do group work.

There are a range of possible benefits that working in a study group can bring to your revision and exam preparation:

■ **Teamwork and support.** Working in a team can engender a spirit of camaraderie between students. You all have a common goal – to do as well in the exams as possible – and this shared objective should ensure that you work together in a supportive and cooperative way. It can also make you feel more confident in knowing that others share your feelings and concerns in advance of the exam. Because the interaction of an effective study group makes it more fun, you can spend more time studying – the better and more valuable it is, the more you will want to do it.

■ **Procrastination killer.** Agreeing to turn up to a study group meeting at a particular time means that students cannot procrastinate (unless they skip the study group completely).

It means that you are more likely to engage actively with your revision. Knowing that other group members are depending on you might also make you more committed to study.

- **Motivation.** An effective study group can help you stay motivated and focused on a topic, even if you find the topic is difficult or, frankly, boring. Interacting and discussing the material with other people will force you to stay focused on the task, rather than just reading the material in a textbook, or re-reading your lecture notes (and then perhaps reading them one final time before losing interest).

- **Learn more efficiently.** A topic that seems utterly baffling to you could be quite clear to someone else in the group. Instead of spending valuable time puzzling over the difficulty yourself, you can simply ask a question and see if anyone can help you. (If you are all stuck though, you will need to seek advice from your lecturer.) Similarly you can feel good about your own knowledge by helping your colleagues when they have difficulties with something that you do understand. Teaching someone else is a good way to learn and to identify gaps in your own knowledge. You may also find that the group may be able to solve a problem together that none of its members would have been able to manage on their own.

- **Improve critical analysis.** Working in a study group will give you a range of perspectives on the material (whereas working alone will only ever give you your own perspective). In discussion, you should be exposed to a variety of viewpoints, which will force you to consider your own personal perspective and therefore help to develop your skills of critical analysis (which are always a key to exam success – see Chapters 8 and 9).

- **Learn new tricks.** Within the study group, you will experience a whole range of different study methods. You might find some new ideas which you can incorporate into your private study; in return you can share your favourite study tips with the group.

- **Fill in the gaps.** Study groups can give you an opportunity to fill the gaps in each other's resources. For instance, you may have missed a lecture or a tutorial but can catch the notes up from one of the other group members. You might also have found an interesting case or article on the topic for the session that you can bring along to discuss.

- **Help your memory.** Discussing topics can make them easier to remember in the exam. You may be able to remember the material by thinking back to the study group session in which you went through it. (See Chapter 5 for more on memory and place.)

- **Informality.** Study groups are much less formal than a lecture or tutorial and most students usually feel more comfortable asking questions in the study group setting. This allows them to find answers to questions without worrying about asking a stupid question.

There are, then, several possible benefits to seeking out and joining a study group. However, if there is no group for you to join, then you will need to set about forming one. The next section will discuss some of the ways in which you might go about it.

◼ Getting a group together

There are all sorts of ways in which study groups can form:

- **Ask your friends.** Most study groups form in quite an informal way between groups of friends from lectures or tutorial groups, or law students living in a shared house or student accommodation.

- **Ask around.** As well as asking your friends, you could simply ask around before or after lectures to see if anyone was interested in working together.

- **Ask a lecturer.** You could see if your lecturer would announce that there are students interested in forming a study group (or groups) and invite anyone interested to come forward. Alternatively, you could see if they knew of any students who have said that they would be interested in working with others.

- **Ask the Student Law Society.** If you have a Student Law Society, it might be able to put students who want to form groups together, or, at least, be able to coordinate introductions.

- **Advertise.** If there is a Law noticeboard, you could put up a simple notice with contact details, or you might post a message on an online student discussion forum or social networking website.

As you can see, there is no excuse for not being able to get a group together if it is something that you really want to try. However, there are some possible pitfalls which you should also bear in mind. Two of the more common are illustrated by Emily's experience:

STUDENT EXPERIENCE

I thought that it would be a really good idea to form a little study group for tort law. A few of us got together and it was all going fine, but then this one girl was really insistent that she wanted to join. We let her, but all she really wanted was for us to do her work for her and never contributed anything to the group. Everyone really ended up resenting doing her work for her, but we never knew how to tell her to stop being a parasite and just leave us alone.

Emily

It is a sad fact of human nature that some people will seek out an easy ride if there is one available. As the interloper in Emily's group demonstrates, there are some that assume that working with others is an easier option than working alone. In actual fact, you should make sure that you do not neglect your own personal study time entirely. There is a balance to be struck between group work and individual work; you might, for example, decide within your group that each of you will go off and prepare something before the group next gets together. The other problem is managing the group to avoid disagreements in the first place or coping with differences that do occur in a constructive and adult fashion: this is sometimes more easily said than done, particularly in the pressured lead up to the exam. It is important, then, to try to set a few simple ground rules before you get going.

Setting the ground rules

In order to keep the group as harmonious as possible, then, it is important to set some ground rules. There is no hard and fast list of what such rules should include, but this section gives you some guidance of the sorts of things that you might want to consider. One of the key points to remember, though, is that since law students are training to use and interpret rules, there is a danger that your group might get bogged down in providing for every eventuality or arguing over the interpretation of particular rules. Keep it simple. The time and place for considering constitutional matters is in your public law revision!

- **Size.** A group with between four and six members seems to be the most effective but smaller or larger groups can also work; a great deal depends on the personality of the group members and their contribution to the group. You should think whether you want the group to expand continually, or to call a halt once the group reaches an optimum size.

- **When to meet.** You will need to decide what time to meet. Is there a time during the day when you are all available? You should certainly not prioritise group working over timetabled lectures or tutorials. Evenings may be easier to arrange, but remember that you will need to eat at some point! Of course, you could always go out to eat together afterwards. (This will help your subconscious mind start to assimilate the material you have covered – see Chapter 5.)

- **Where to meet.** It is preferable to meet somewhere like a group working area in your library, or in study rooms in the library, law department or student union, rather that in someone's room or house. You may also be able to book rooms through your department: if in doubt, ask one of the support staff who should be able to help.

- **Length and frequency of sessions.** It is usually more productive to have more frequent shorter sessions (that is, sessions that are more intensive and focused) than longer meetings, which run a much greater risk of drifting off into unproductive activity. If you plan a long study session, make sure you include time for breaks. It is probably best to keep sessions no longer than one-and-a-half to two hours.

- **What to bring.** You should decide what materials to bring to the meetings. You might not need six copies of the same textbook, for instance, so you could ask some members to bring statute books, others one of your set texts and others a different book all together. Depending on the time of the meeting, you might want to have snacks, biscuits or pizza to keep you going, but remember that the purpose of the meeting is study, not socialise. You should certainly avoid alcohol during the meeting.

- **What to do if there are problems.** You should agree that if any of the members thinks that the group is not working for them, then they should be free to drop out without any fear of causing offence. You should also agree that the group should be able to express any negative views about the contribution (or otherwise!) of its members in an adult fashion. If, as in Emily's experience, the group feels that one member is leeching off the others, then they should be able to say that. In most cases, the criticised student will either spring into action and start contributing properly or be so embarrassed that they decide to leave the group. However, be careful not to victimise people.

■ What to do

Assuming that you are a member of a study group with a clear set of ground rules, then the next step is to think about the activities that you might like to try in your sessions.

Before that, though, you need to agree the topic and purpose of each session in advance so that everyone can think about it and prepare for it. Be careful to keep the scope of your sessions sensible and try not to take on too much or you run the risk of losing focus: a study group that decides that the aim of its next session is to 'revise land law' stands a much smaller chance of being effective compared to one that sets out to 'revise adverse possession'. You might also want to decide what you could do after the session as a reward for your efforts.

Once you have a topic to cover, you should next aim to share the workload of revision amongst the members of the group. You could:

■ Agree that each person will prepare a set of revision notes on a particular topic and distribute these amongst the group. With four people in a group, you would have notes on eight topics even though you had only prepared two sets of notes yourself. Obviously, you are dependent on the work of others, which is another reason to ensure that you trust students who join the group to do the work and to do it to a reasonable quality.

■ Select a topic for discussion or a task to complete as a group and either record the activity or nominate someone to take notes, so that you have a record of what was said and done. For example, you could agree to spend an hour working out what the key elements of negligence are and what cases should be used to support the main principles.

■ Prepare templates and quizzes to share with the group or write practice answers and compare them with the rest of the group. One group once spent a great deal of time making a version of Trivial Pursuit that replaced the usual categories with the six subjects that they were studying in their second year which they then played at every opportunity. It was so good that other students offered to pay to take part. This shows that you can make revision into an enjoyable activity, but do be wary of devising activities that take too much time to set up and organise. These students came up with the idea at Christmas and spread the writing of questions across several months.

■ Find questions from past exam papers that are relevant to the topic for the session and come up with answer plans between you.

- Go through various journal articles on the topic and agree the key points from each of them. Make lists of similarities and differences between alternative academic viewpoints.

Finally, it is important to remember that if you get to a point where you are collectively stuck, then you should seek help from your lecturer who should be willing to assist.

Lecturer viewpoint

I always like questions that come from study groups. If a group of students still don't get a topic after working together, then it might mean that I didn't explain it clearly enough in the lectures or that it might need more focus in tutorials. This feedback helps me make my course better for the next year, so of course I'll try to sort their problem out.

■ What not to do

There are some common pitfalls that can occur when working in a group:

- **Neglecting your own study.** You need to make sure that you strike a balance between the needs of your own private study and supporting the other members of the study group. Make sure that you get as much out of the group as you put in. Working in a study group is not a soft option or an alternative to taking responsibility for your own learning.

- **Bringing each other down.** Be careful not to let the session degenerate into a discussion of how difficult things are, your negative perceptions of the course, your lecturers or your fellow students. If you get a sense that this is happening, try to snap the rest of the group out of it and channel your energies into doing something positive.

- **Wasting time.** Sometimes it is easier to chat about almost anything rather than studying. You need to focus on what you are trying to achieve together.

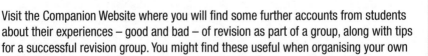

www.pearsoned.co.uk/lawexpress

■ To find out more …

Visit the Companion Website where you will find some further accounts from students about their experiences – good and bad – of revision as part of a group, along with tips for a successful revision group. You might find these useful when organising your own revision groups.

NOTES

Memorising

Revision checklist

Topics covered in this chapter:

- [ ] Understanding how your memory works
- [ ] The importance of sleep and the subconscious
- [ ] Methods for making material memorable
- [ ] Categorising information
- [ ] Triggering memory by senses
- [ ] Associating memories with places
- [ ] Using mnemonics
- [ ] The difference between recall and understanding

■ Introduction

One of the most common laments of a law student, particularly in the run up to exams, is 'there is so much to remember'. Law students worry that their memory will not be sufficiently effective for them to be successful in their exams. While it is true that law is made up of a large number of cases, statutes, theories, arguments and principles, there are some techniques that you can use in order to make material memorable. In order to do this, it is useful to understand a little about how your memory works before getting on to some suggestions that you might try for training it before the exam. You should realise that your memory can be improved and this ought to quell some of the fears that you will just go blank in the exam itself.

■ Understanding your memory

There have been many studies conducted on the functioning of the human memory. At this stage, the detail of the studies themselves is not that important. What is more important, though, is how the findings relate to your exam preparation.

Many people describe their memory as being like an enormous mental filing cabinet full of folders in which information, in the form of individual memories, is stored away. Others think of memory as a neural supercomputer in their head. However, medical and psychological experts now believe that memory is far more complex than those two simple conceptualisations, and that it is a brain-wide process, rather than just being the job of one particular part of the brain.

Memory and sleep

Does this experience sound familiar?

STUDENT EXPERIENCE

If I revise in the morning, then I usually can't remember a word of it by the evening. But the next morning, when I come to revise again, it seems easier again. I don't understand why I can remember things some of the time, but not all of the time.

Archana

There is a simple explanation for this: *recall improves after one night's sleep*. So, on the same day, Archana's ability to recall the information she had revised in the morning was not as good as it was after a night's sleep. While we sleep, the part of the brain that stores

Figure 5.1 The hippocampus and the cortex

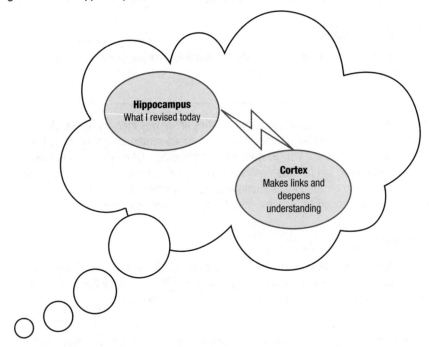

recent information (the hippocampus) 'tells' the part of the brain responsible for deeper levels of information (the cortex) what has happened that day. Then, the cortex makes sense of that day's experiences and attempts to make sense of everything, deepening understanding and making links between recent experience and deeper, stored experience.

In other words, any information from the day that the cortex thinks is worth remembering gets assimilated into the brain overnight.

So, if the power of recall is best after a good night's sleep, why not leave all your revision until the night before the exam? This strategy may have worked for you as a child facing a spelling test the next day, even if your parents thought you were being lazy. However, there is a qualitative difference between an undergraduate law exam and a seven-year-old's list of tricky words to learn. Law exams are harder. You need a much deeper level of understanding and, in order to give yourself the best chance of exam success, you need to be able to link material together. Remember that one of the jobs of the sleeping brain is to make links between long-term memories: if you only give your brain one night to make sense of the entire course, then that is not enough.

It would also be a bad idea to record your notes and play them back while you are sleeping. Although this method is sometimes used, it is better to get some proper sleep to allow the brain to do its thing rather than bombarding it subconsciously with new information.

Memory and the subconscious

STUDENT EXPERIENCE

I'd been struggling to understand equity and trusts for months and then, all of a sudden, it seemed to make a lot more sense.

Lauren

Lauren's experience can also be explained in terms of the way memory works. *Our subconscious mind works on material even when we are awake.* So, not only had her sleeping brain had plenty of time to work on understanding, and making links between pieces of information, but her subconscious was also hard at work when she was awake. Taking frequent rest breaks to do something completely different can give the subconscious some time to sift through and process information, as can simply 'mulling it all over'.

EXAM TIP

Make sure that you get enough sleep and take frequent breaks while revising. Give your mind time to process and absorb the information that you want it to remember. Allow yourself plenty of time to try to commit a topic to memory.

Given that the passage of time also helps recall, it follows that it is a very risky strategy to try to cram revision into the night before the exam. It is also much less likely that you will remember material learnt on the day of the exam, as neither the sleeping or subconscious brain will have had much opportunity to process the material. Although a very small number of people have their brains wired in such a way that they have incredible powers of short-term recollection just before exams (including one of the authors of this book!) it would be quite bold to take a chance on this strategy working for you. Take your time over revision, take plenty of breaks and get enough sleep.

Memory and diet

Most people will have heard the saying that 'fish is good for the brain'. Indeed, back in the 1950s, all schoolchildren in England were given a daily dose of cod liver oil. There is a wealth of research that suggests omega-3 and omega-6 fatty acids (which are found in oily fish such as mackerel, salmon and sardines as well as other foods like walnuts and kiwi fruit) improve concentration and memory. The right balance of these two types of fatty acids is important for the healthy functioning of many parts of the body: they are also claimed to help against depression (which might be useful if the thought of the exams starts getting you down).

It has also been claimed that water helps memory: even slight levels of dehydration have been shown to affect memory adversely.

Memory and lapse of time

While it might have sounded like great news that your powers of recall will be at their best after only one night's sleep, the bad news is that your ability to remember will decline after the first revision. Therefore, you have to make sure that you top-up your revision periodically and, with multiple revisions, your ability to recall the material should improve.

Figure 5.2 Memory increases with multiple revisions

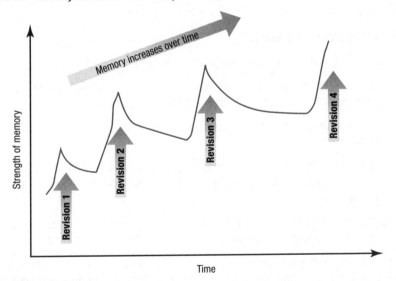

You also need to make sure that the information is *memorable*. This is because the brain can sometimes work against you. It is excellent at filtering out trivia or things that are familiar or seemingly unimportant. If you are not concentrating on something it is unlikely to register. Have you ever had the experience of re-reading a set of notes and just thinking 'yes, I know all this, just about' and then skimming the remainder? There is nothing that you are doing to make the information memorable – that is, able to be remembered. There are various techniques that you can try to trick your brain into making material memorable which we will cover in the next section.

Making material memorable

It is much easier to recall things that you have understood. This is why it is important to review your syllabus and to weed out topics that have never made any sense to you. If you have not grasped them by the time that the revision period starts, then it is probably too late and require too great an investment in time to try to get to grips with them now.

 Try this

Does it *really* make sense?

Take a piece of material that you are trying to revise and do the following.

1 Does it seem to make sense to you on a first read (or re-read) through? As you skim it, do you get the gist of its meaning? Be honest with yourself!

2 Write an outline of the material. Can you do this without constantly re-checking your notes?

3 Can you apply the material to a past essay or problem question? Or, if you have set up some self-test questions, or quiz questions, can you answer them reasonably well?

4 Can you explain it to one of your friends, or a patient member of your family? If they have questions, can you answer them sufficiently clearly – or at all?

If you are struggling to make sense of the material, try re-reading it again with more focus. Try discussing it with someone who knows the subject – maybe one of your friends, or a willing lecturer – or use some of the other revision activities covered in Chapter 3.

Once you have worked out what material it is that you need to be able to recall, you can start planning your strategies for remembering it.

Memory is triggered by *association* (remember the role of the cortex in making mental links between things) so it can really help your revision if you vary your ways of making associations. Many different memory training techniques work by linking new information to very familiar things that the brain has already learnt, such as music, people, colour, stories, experiences and places.

Memory and organisation

If material is well organised in the first place, then the brain finds it much easier to remember. Also, if you impose an organised structure on the information which tells the brain to remember it in the way that *you* want to, then it will minimise the chances of the brain imposing its own unhelpful structure.

 Try this

Categorising material

Try to remember the following list of nine terms. Give yourself a minute to commit the list to memory and then see how many you can recall. It does not matter what order you remember them in.

- Breach of duty
- Intention permanently to deprive
- Appropriation
- Duty of care
- Belonging to another
- Causation
- Property
- Remoteness of damage
- Dishonesty

How did you get on? If you realised that the lists actually contained the elements of the offence of theft in criminal law and the elements of negligence in tort, you may have quickly reordered them into two separate lists in a more familiar and logical order:

Theft

- Dishonesty
- Appropriation

- Property
- Belonging to another
- Intention permanently to deprive

Negligence

- Duty of care
- Breach of duty
- Causation
- Remoteness of damage

This is a very simple example which demonstrates that categorising information under key words or labels can make it easier to recall.

There are many ways in which you could organise your material:

- **Put it into categories.** As shown in the example above, one way of organising material is to put it into categories. You can divide material into topic areas which could be triggered by a key word or label for each area.

- **Make lists.** You can make lists of just about anything: cases, treaty provisions, sections of statute. If you have a list of numbered items to remember, then it is also useful to remember how many items there are on the list and try to memorise each item with its corresponding number. The example demonstrated the five elements of theft or the four elements of negligence.

- **Condense and consolidate.** You should aim to take the notes that you have made during lectures, in preparation for seminars, and as part of your private study and condense them into a more concise and memorable set of key points. Condensing your notes is an important part of the revision process. Not only does it produce a set of concise points that can be committed to memory, the actual process of filtering and recording information will contribute to your understanding of the material as you make decisions about the significance of different points and the relationship between them. Some students like to then condense their condensed notes, so that they ultimately end up with a single page that covers a vast range of material and which triggers recollection of the detail behind it.

- **Impose a structure.** You can structure your material by identifying the most significant areas and breaking each of these down into sub-points. You can then organise this onto a page of revision notes that best suits your own particular memory strengths – some people find it easier to remember information in linear notes, others in flowcharts or diagrams and some in mind maps.

In essence, it is easier for the brain to retrieve information that has been stored in a structured way so you will find it easier to recall information in the exam if you categorised it during the revision process. If no natural categories seem to exist, create categories by using techniques such as making up stories with the case names or creating acronyms from the initial letters of key points. You can also create categories in your brain simply by the way that you set out your revision notes on paper. The following note-taking techniques can be very effective in helping you to organise information in a way that makes it more easily memorable. Whatever approach to note-taking you adopt, the most important thing to remember is that they should be useful to you.

Linear notes

Linear revision notes use blocks of text, often separated by headings or bullet points with key points that can be emphasised by highlighting or underlining. The potential pitfall of linear notes in relation to revision lies in the fact that students often replicate their lecture notes, resulting in almost duplicate reams of revision notes that have very little value.

STUDENT EXPERIENCE

I used to spend all of my revision time making notes that I would then keep reading and rewriting to try and fix them in my mind but it was never that successful. Then I found that if I condensed each topic to a series of key words and cases, I could picture how the layout of the page looked in the exam and I had no difficulty in remembering things.

Janet

Linear notes make an excellent starting point for revision but they do tend to be less memorable than some other methods of recording information. If you do favour linear notes, try to reduce them every time that you produce them so that you condense each topic to a series of words and phrases that enable you to recall the main points and key authorities.

Flowcharts

Flowcharts build on linear notes to include an indication of the relationship that different points have to each other. These are generally more valuable as a memory aid as you need to think carefully about structure and categorisation in order to produce from your lecture notes.

By noting the relationships between different points, you are imposing a structure on the information that you are storing in your brain and so retrieval should be easier. Figure 5.3 shows an example of a flowchart that deals with non-fatal offences against the person in criminal law.

Figure 5.3 Flowchart of non-fatal offences

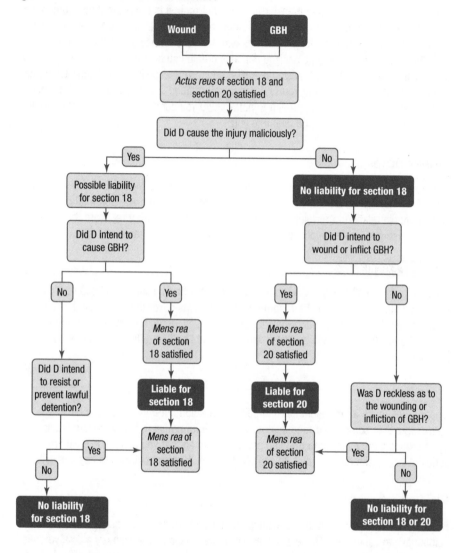

Mind maps

Mind maps (also called concept maps or spider diagrams) are a way of recording not just the key words, ideas, and concepts but also the links between them. This reflects the way that memory operates: your mind automatically makes associations between the different pieces of information stored in your memory and mind maps provide a way to depict information that shows these links and associations. Many students report that they find it easier to recall information from mind maps than they do from linear notes because of the visual image involved: in other words, they can picture the shape of the map and then recollect the information that it contains follows. The ease with which they can be recalled make mind maps an excellent revision tool.

There is software available that will help you to produce mind maps, but it is very simple to do using a pen and paper. Simply draw a shape in the centre of a piece of paper and write the name of the topic in it. Many students use a rectangle or circle as their central shape but some students like to use shapes that reflect the nature of the topic. As each major theme emerges, draw a line that runs from the central shape and write the name of the theme at the end of the line. Repeat this for other major themes. Figure 5.4 shows a mind map for vicarious liability in tort.

You will see that the four 'big' concepts are: the meaning of 'employee'; that a tort must be committed; that it must be done in the course of employment and indemnities. More lines run from these ideas to create links to particular aspects of this idea. For example, 'employee' divides into three tests: the control test, the economic reality test and the organisation/integration test. You can use images, symbols or colours to help points to stand out and stick in your mind. For example, you will see a bus next to the cases involving 'course of employment' as many of these were transport cases. There is an exclamation mark next to the branch that says that a tort must have been committed, since this is an area that many students overlook. You can also add notes to supplement the structure – there is a note next to the economic reality test to remind you that it is the one that is used most frequently. Many of the points have a key case or statute next to them. Also, in this example, there are numbers which illustrate how many points follow – so there are four elements to consider in vicarious liability, three in relation to the definition of 'employee' and so forth. This will help you if you like to remember lists of things.

Memory and senses

Memories are also triggered by senses. You should engage your senses when revising as this may also help your powers of recollection in the exam room.

Figure 5.4 Vicarious liability mind map

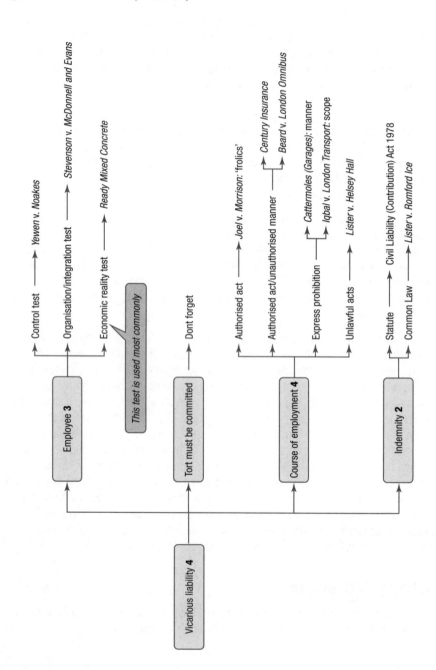

Visual memory

Visual memory is concerned with 'seeing' information in your mind's eye. If you are able to recollect whereabouts on a page a certain piece of information was written then this suggests that you have a good visual memory. As such, there are various things that you can do to develop your visual memory further:

- **Make each page of revision notes look different.** Try using different coloured paper for different topics: for instance, red for criminal offences and green for defences.

- **Present your material in different ways.** You should try a combination of diagrams, charts, flowcharts, mind maps, pictures, sketches or even cartoons to depict the material you are trying to remember. A picture can be particularly effective in helping to remember case law. You do not have to be a brilliant artist to capture the idea as Figure 5.5 will demonstrate. It illustrates (simply) the key facts from *Scott* v. *St Katherine's Docks Co* (1865) concerning the three conditions that must be satisfied to ensure the availability of *res ipsa loquitur* in tort. In this case, the claimant was injured by a sack of sugar which fell from a crane operated by the defendants. The court held that a claimant will be assisted by *res ipsa loquitur* if: the thing causing the damage is under the control of the defendant or someone for whose negligence the defendant is responsible; the cause of the accident is unknown; and the accident is such as would not normally occur without negligence.

- **Revise with visual memory in mind.** Concentrate on where material is situated on the page, as well as its content.

- **Use colours and shapes within your notes.** You may, for instance, highlight all case names in yellow and statutes in orange or link points with different styles of arrow.

Figure 5.5 *Res ipsa loquitur* case picture

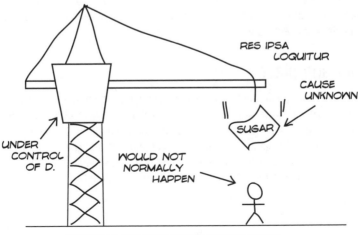

SCOTT V. ST. KATHERINE DOCKS (1865)

Motor memory

The ideal of linking an idea to the senses of feeling or doing is often used by hypnotherapists. For instance, the brain can be programmed to recall a sense of calmness when pinching thumb and forefinger together, so that, if stressed, all you have to do is do the pinching movement and the positive memory will be triggered. If the act of reproducing material itself seems to be the factor that helps you to remember it, rather than visualising it in your mind's eye, then you could try some of the following ideas:

- **Write, write and write again.** The act of writing (or typing) material repeatedly might help it to stick.

- **Move your finger around the page as you revise.** If you use your finger to trace through a paragraph, or navigate a diagram or flowchart, the sense of motion can help your motor memory.

- **Mutter it to yourself.** If you mutter the material quietly to yourself, then the act of doing this might enable you to recall it in the exam – although you must not disturb others, so do be *very* quiet.

Hearing memory

Finally, you may find that you can recall information better by repeating it to yourself, or remembering where you heard it. If this is the case, your hearing (or auditory) memory may be strong and you might benefit from these suggestions:

- **Use music.** Revise each topic to music (although try to keep the music to the background to give yourself enough head space to concentrate on the material at hand) – the music could then form the association to the material. Alternatively, if you are particularly creative, you could make up a song or jingle about the topic.

- **Record and rewind.** Record yourself saying the material out loud and then play it back to yourself on your phone or MP3 player. You could then explain the topic to your friends (see Chapter 4 on working with others).

Memory and place

Another way of recalling information is to associate it with particular places. If you vary the location where you revise, you may be able to picture the place where you were and link this to the material. For instance, you might have revised offer and acceptance in your room, consideration in the library and intention to create legal relations sitting in the park. These associations can also help you to remember material. You might also be able to link specific topics to the location of a particular lecture or tutorial and visualise it in your memory.

I was really struggling to answer a fourth question in my crime exam so I was reading and re-reading the questions trying to think of something to write. One of the essays was on consent and non-fatal offences and the only thing I could remember about that was that we all pretended not to know the facts of one of the cases in the tutorial because they were embarrassing. Eventually a girl called Bev explained them so graphically that even the lecturer went red. Just remembering that incident took me right back to the tutorial so that I could picture where I was sitting and where Bev was in the room and, as I visualised it, all the discussion came flooding back into my mind. I ended up writing about four-and-a-half pages which was pretty good because I had thought that I wouldn't even be able to attempt a fourth question.

Janet

This ability to visualise a location and use this as a trigger for particular memories can be useful to your revision. Make the most of this by revising each topic in a particular place. If you were revising in the garden and had a list of cases relating to acceptance in contract law, you might revise *Adams* v. *Lindsell* by a rose bush, *Henthorn* v. *Fraser* facing the greenhouse, *Brinkibon* v. *Stahag Stahl* behind the shed and *Holwell Securities* v. *Hughes* under the apple tree. In the exam, you can visualise your position in the garden and this should help to trigger the associated memory.

Another link between information and place can be achieved by spreading our materials around your room or house. You could put a list of cases on the fridge, some key statutory provisions by the airing cupboard and a list of key points by the kettle. Again, making the association between *where* the information was and *what* it was can ease recollection.

Mnemonics

A mnemonic is a technique to aid memory which forms an association between the material we want to remember and something else, such as a very short poem, an image, or a phrase or special (or nonsense) word, that is easier for us to remember.

Many people learned the colours of the rainbow by remembering 'Richard Of York Gave Battle In Vain': this can be applied to the law as well. For example, going back to the elements of negligence we mentioned earlier – that is duty of care, breach of duty, causation and remoteness, you could associate the first letter of each with a simple phrase like this:

- Dog
- Bites
- Cause
- Rabies.

This is particularly effective if you couple it with the image of a negligent owner letting their rabid dog off the leash: an extra association between the mnemonic and its topic. The difficulty with this approach is that it can take quite a long time to come up with a phrase that makes sense although, once it is done, remembering it is quite easy. 'Dog Bites Cause Rabies' took about twenty minutes, via 'nearly' options with dirty bedding and rashes, and one that was not suitable for publication – although having said that, if you are so inclined, rude or controversial mnemonics often stick in the memory particularly well.

Some students also remember material by coming up with a mnemonic narrative or story that combines elements of that material. The story does not have to make sense: again, the more unusual, ridiculous or atmospheric the story, the more likely it is to be remembered. Of course, many cases have memorable stories attached to them (although you will usually think of them as the facts of the case, they are, if you think about it, the story of what happened before the case got to court).

Example: Silly story

This is an excerpt from a silly story that combines the names and facts of cases that are relevant to the coincidence of *actus reus* and *mens rea* in criminal law. The names of the cases are in bold and the facts are written in italics.

Thabo Meli was driving to **church** with his friend, the **miller**, when he saw a *tramp* and Joan **Collins** *running from a burning house*. He was so distracted that he was not paying attention to the road and he *ran over a policeman's foot*.

The advantage of creating short scenarios like this is that they can be easily visualised and will prompt your memory.

Another method that can be useful is to take the initial letters of a list of cases or key terms and create a word or short phrase out of them. You might need to use the first two letters in some cases to ensure you have enough vowels to make a word. If you struggle to create anagrams, then try using an online anagram generator such as the one at www.wordsmith.org.

Dates and numbers

Dates of cases or statutes and individual provision numbers (for students who do not get to refer to statutory material in their exams) are one of the biggest concerns for law students. They are often the hardest things to remember, and there is no magic formula for being able to do so. What you should do, however, is use a combination of the techniques covered earlier in this chapter to work out the best way of recalling that information for you, along with some of these suggestions:

- **Repeat, reuse, recycle.** Dates often only stick through repetition. Whenever you think of a statute or a case always try to think of it with its year, rather than stopping after the name of the statute or case itself: so think of 'the Unfair Contract Terms Act 1977' rather than 'the Unfair Contract Terms Act'. This will help the date to stick.

■ **Associate with a memorable date.** This can sometimes help. For instance, one of the authors always remembers the date of the *Practice Statement* concerning judicial precedent in the House of Lords as being 1966 because England won the World Cup in that year and wished that it had set a precedent. Incidentally, this also helps them to remember the date of another key precedent case (*Young* v. *Bristol Aeroplane*) as 1944, because, like 1966, this ends in a double digit.

■ **Associate with other memorable numbers.** For example, your aunt may live at number 9, and you could imagine her house being burgled (burglary is found in section 9 of the Theft Act 1968). Other numbers have special connotations that might help you to make associations: 7 is considered lucky while 13 is unlucky, 18 is the year that you are allowed to drink in pubs. For instance, you might think that you were quite unlucky if someone came to repair your washing machine, but instead caused it to flood your house: the good news is that reasonable care and skill is required under section 13 (unlucky) of the Supply of Goods and Services Act 1982.

■ **Associate with rhyme.** You can also make rhyming associations with section numbers: for example, burglary is fine (section **9**, Theft Act 1968) and robbery is great (section **8**).

Information and understanding

The techniques described in the chapter so far are designed to help you to recall information in the exam room. However, one caveat here is that recollection of information is not the same as understanding it. You need to understand both the significance of that information and the topic as a whole in order to do well. If all that was being tested was your ability to recall information, then law would only be examined by multiple-choice questions.

 Lecturer viewpoint

I had one student who told me that her revision was going swimmingly. She said that she had the names and dates of 50 key cases committed to memory. I asked her about the legal principles associated with some of the cases and she hadn't got a clue.

Hopefully, you can see the distinction between knowledge (recollection of facts) and understanding (being able to use them to demonstrate your ability to use the law to answer essays or problem questions). In order to do this, you need to deepen your knowledge of the subject, so that its recollection almost becomes second nature and your mental faculties are focused on using the material to address the particular question at hand. It can take a long time to reach this point, but it is key that you focus on the key information required and then use it as actively as possible: working with information, selecting it, sifting it and applying it will help to build this foundation of knowledge that underpins deeper understanding. Also, the more you know about a subject, the quicker it will be for you to fit new information into it, so the growth of knowledge almost becomes self-perpetuating.

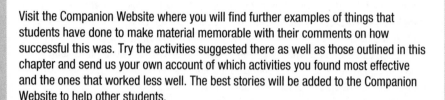

www.pearsoned.co.uk/lawexpress

■ To find out more ...

Visit the Companion Website where you will find further examples of things that students have done to make material memorable with their comments on how successful this was. Try the activities suggested there as well as those outlined in this chapter and send us your own account of which activities you found most effective and the ones that worked less well. The best stories will be added to the Companion Website to help other students.

NOTES

Final preparation

6

Revision checklist

Topics covered in this chapter:

- [ ] Selecting material to revise if time is short
- [ ] Suggestions for last minute revision activities
- [ ] Ensuring that you are administratively well-prepared
- [ ] Dealing with pre-exam nerves

■ Introduction

If you have paced your study and revision, you should be feeling relatively confident as the day of the exam itself approaches. However, there is a possibility that you have arrived at this chapter as you feel ill-prepared and stressed as a result. Perhaps you have only just got hold of this book and the exam is tomorrow. This chapter will give you some practical advice on steps that you can take in the final run up to the exam, and a few pointers on what you could (but also should not) do as a last resort at the very last minute. It will also give you some guidance on dealing with pre-exam nerves.

■ Emergency revision

 Lecturer viewpoint

Students often cram the night before and lecturers always say they shouldn't. Although cramming might get a student through the exam, they shouldn't forget that they are storing up problems for later courses, as cramming can give short-term knowledge but doesn't leave enough time for proper understanding.

If your revision strategy is entirely based around cramming, then it is quite unlikely that you will be able to demonstrate sufficient understanding and perform the level of critical analysis required for a first-class result, but having some knowledge in your short-term memory can certainly save you from failing an exam. Of course, it is better going into an exam with some knowledge – albeit limited – rather than none whatsoever. However, there are a few students who find that they work best of all under pressure.

STUDENT EXPERIENCE

I always leave it till the last minute. The stress of knowing that the exam is looming really focuses my mind. But every time I get my results, I wonder if I would have done better if I'd started earlier.

Matt

Although you might be one of those students who does perform best under extreme pressure, you may – as Matt did – still get lingering doubts that you might well have performed better had you allowed yourself a longer and more structured period of exam preparation.

Sometimes students will try to find ways to avoid responsibility for the situation they find themselves in:

I usually stay up all night before an exam. My results aren't always as good as I hoped for, but that's probably because I'm pretty shattered by the time I get to the exam room.

Tom

Tom's experience is quite common among students. It is actually a good example of something that psychologists call 'self-handicapping'. By leaving things to the last minute, even if you fail, you can blame your failure on your procrastination or your tiredness. This helps you hide from facing up to the fact that you might not actually be very good at the subject. Conversely, if you do manage to get through the exam, you can say that you managed to do so in spite of leaving everything to the last minute, or being tired, so you can make yourself feel even better about your ability. So, cramming can be driven by a need to protect your self-esteem, but it is not actually going to help you in the long run. Studies have shown that the knowledge of your own self-deception makes you more likely to self-handicap in the future. It is a vicious circle and if you end up cramming just because you have been putting off starting revision, then you are not giving yourself your best chance.

If you have arrived at this point, though, all is not yet lost. Here are some suggestions as to what you could do in the limited time available. However, for future exams, you would be well-advised to start earlier so that you do not find yourself in this position again. Once you have got your exam out of the way, look back at Chapter 2 for some advice on revision planning and try to be more organised next time around.

Spread your revision over multiple topics

Unless the format of the paper is really unusual (see Chapter 1 for an overview of question paper styles) then you will be required to answer more than one question. It follows that, even with limited time left, it would be a foolish idea only to concentrate on revising one topic to the exclusion of everything else. This would certainly limit the number of questions that you could realistically tackle.

Even in an emergency situation – such as having less than 24 hours before the exam starts and not having started your revision – you should always revise enough topics for the number of questions *plus one spare* in case one of your crammed topics does not come up, or that you cannot face the particular question that has been asked about it. So, for example, you should aim to revise five topics for a four-question exam.

Of course, if you go into such an exam with only five topics under your belt, there is always a risk that you will still be short, or that one of your chosen topics arises in combination with something that you had not covered. This is just one of the risks you have to accept if you leave starting your revision until the last minute. However, it is preferable to aim to revise 'number of questions plus one' topics, rather than double the number of topics, or everything on the syllabus, as, in a limited fixed time, your knowledge would become increasingly superficial the more topics you tried to cram. You should make a trade off between number of topics and depth of knowledge, so that you do not end up spreading your valuable revision time too thinly between too many topics.

Count up how many hours there are until the exam starts and make a realistic assessment of how many of those hours you can spend on revision. You should use every spare moment effectively: add an extra hour or two of revision to the day (either by getting up and getting started earlier, by finishing and going to bed later, or a combination of the two), but make sure that you allow yourself some time to sleep as this is important in helping material lodge in your memory (see Chapter 5). Break the remaining hours available down into one-and-a-half hour revision slots and allocate a specific task to each session. However, be careful that you do not fall into the common trap of overrunning.

STUDENT EXPERIENCE

I had my contract law exam coming up and hadn't started revising. I knew that there was almost always a question on contract formation, so I revised offer, acceptance and consideration until I thought I'd got them. At least I knew I could do one question. But there wasn't much time left to do anything else, so I ended up skipping through a few other topics. I got 63 on the formation question, but not much on the others, and ended up failing the exam overall. I'll try never to get in that position again, but if I do, I'll remember to spread my revision out.

Holly

Be strict with yourself and do not allow your revision time per topic to overrun. If you do, there is a risk that, like Holly, you will keep working on your first topic until you are happy with it and then suddenly realise that you have insufficient time to cover much else. This can have dire consequences for your overall exam performance as one good question out of four will never be enough to get you through.

Last minute revision activities

There are a whole range of revision activities in Chapter 3 that can help you to prepare for your exams. However, when time is short, you may need to take a different approach. One thing that is common to all effective revision is that it should be active: that is, you should do things as well as passively reading (and re-reading) information. This helps you to memorise more effectively (see Chapter 8) even if you are in a hurry.

One approach to last minute revision is shown in Figure 6.1.

Figure 6.1 Last minute revision: one possible approach

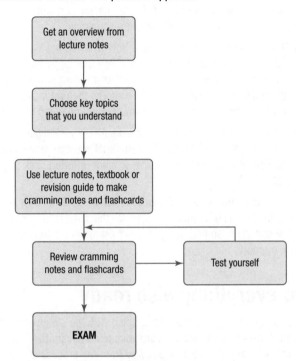

The key steps in this process are as follows:

- **Get an overview from lecture notes.** Assuming that you attended lectures regularly, you should have some notes to look over. If there are some gaps in your lecture notes, see if you can get copies from another student. The content of the lectures is closely linked to the content of the exam: even if you have further reading or non-lectured material that was covered in tutorials, lecturers tend to focus on the key topics in lectures.

- **Choose key topics that you understand.** As you go through your lecture notes, try to pick out the most important material. Write up key cases, statutes and legal principles into a set of cramming notes or on note cards. Not only will this distil the lecture notes, but will also help you identify the main material that you need to know. You will also build up a useful (and easily portable) set of flashcards. The process of rewriting may also help you memorise the content (see Chapter 5).

- **Use your textbook or a revision guide.** As well as using your lecture notes, you should also scan the key sections of your set textbook and add any useful new information you find to your cramming or flashcards. Be careful not to spend too long on this task: its purpose is not for you to copy out everything in the textbook but rather to identify the most important points and focus on them. You should also consider getting a copy of a good revision guide for the subject. The *Law Express* series (of which this book is, of course, a part) is specifically designed to help you quickly to relate all the reading and study throughout your course specifically to exam situations.

- **Review your flashcards or cramming notes.** Now that you have a set of notes and flashcards, you should go through them quickly. If you are happy that you understand a certain point – and, more importantly, can remember it – then move on to the next one. If, however, you are uncertain about any of the material then refer back to your lecture notes, textbook or revision guide and update your cramming notes or cards.

- **Test yourself.** Having checked (and double-checked) your understanding, it is time to start testing yourself. See how much of the material you can remember. Challenge yourself to write it down as quickly as possible without referring back to your notes. Keep as active as possible.

- **Review all your cramming notes or flashcards: one last time.** Just before the exam, flip through your flashcards or cramming notes. Do this even if you are confident that you have memorised them, so that everything is fresh in your mind and, hopefully, in your short-term memory.

Getting everything else ready

Learning, understanding and revising material coupled with the stress of taking an exam is probably enough to worry about. However, last minute administrative hiccups can cause further stress that may take your focus away from the process of revision and can adversely impact upon your performance.

STUDENT EXPERIENCE

I'd spent the last week before my land law exam getting as much into my head as I possibly could. I felt quite good when I turned up at the exam hall, even though I knew I'd been a bit last minute. Then I realised that I'd left my statute book on my desk at home and I felt sick. It really put me off the rest of the exam and I didn't do nearly as well as I hoped I would.

Matt

- **Know where you are going and think about getting there.** You should make sure that you know exactly where the exam is being held and how long it will take you to get there. If you are driving, double check parking arrangements – is there adequate student parking? Is it free? If not, how much will it cost? If you need to park in a pay-and-display, make sure that you have enough change for the machine. Whether you are using public or private transport, make sure you allow some additional time for delays. If you are walking from student accommodation, allow enough time not to have to run!

- **Make any other arrangements.** If you have child care or other such arrangements to make, then make them a week or more before the exam so that you can forget about them.

- **Get everything you need ready.** Unlike Matt, make sure that you have everything you need for the exam. Check the rules for your particular institution to make sure that everything you take into the exam room is not on the prohibited list. If you need to leave a bag somewhere, make sure that it only contains items that are replaceable and do not under any circumstances leave valuables in it. This is not meant to say that students (or invigilators) are common thieves: more a recognition of the fact that it is quite easy to pick up the wrong bag in the immediate aftermath of an exam. Make sure that you have some reliable means of timekeeping, statute books and materials (where permitted), spare pens and your student ID card. You should also take a bottle of water to sip and your favourite sweets, if they are permitted and not irritatingly noisy to unwrap.

- **Emergency communications.** You should also programme the examination emergency number into your phone (this may be somewhere central within the University, or within the law school) in case there are unavoidable delays on the way to the exam. It is better that you inform the University as soon as possible if you are delayed.

Visit the Companion Website for a downloadable checklist that you can use to make sure that you are properly prepared.

Dealing with pre-exam nerves

There are a multitude of reasons that make students worried about exams, but most of these can be categorised as either lack of revision time, that your mind will go completely blank in the exam, or that your ability to work is paralysed by a fear of failure or that your answers will be imperfect in some way. The key point to remember is to *stay positive*: try not to be frightened of your nerves, use them to help you focus on the task in hand. At the very least, remember that there is actually life after exams.

If you are concerned that you have left yourself insufficient revision time, then the suggestions for last minute revision in this chapter should allay some of those fears to a certain extent – as should the more mechanical process of making sure that you are well organised before the exam. That just leaves the two other categories: a blank mind and fear of failure.

Blank mind

There are a few things that you can do to reboot your mind if it goes blank during the exam:

- **Stay calm.** Breathing too quickly (or hyperventilating) is considered by some to be a symptom of a panic attack and as a cause by others. Rapid breathing and panic are certainly very closely linked. If you feel yourself beginning to panic and breathing rapidly, take a few deep breaths or hold your breath for as long as you can (comfortably) to 'reset' your breathing.

My mind went utterly blank in my criminal law exam and I couldn't remember a thing. I could feel myself beginning to panic, so I took a few deep breaths and calmed down. It was only then that it all started coming back to me. Of course I knew the material really, but I got so worked up that all I was thinking about was how awful criminal law was and whether I'd fail so badly that I wouldn't even be offered a resit. It didn't leave any room for homicide offences.

Julianne

- **Work from the basic principles.** If the question seems complicated, start with the easier part of the answer to get yourself started on the question. For instance, a problem question on remoteness in negligence would still require you to discuss the less contentious issues of, say, the existence of a duty of care, whether a breach of duty has occurred as a result of the defendant not having reached the required standard of care in the circumstances, and whether the breach of duty caused the loss or damage suffered.

- **Re-read the question.** If the question seems unfathomable at first sight, then read it again – more slowly – and look for words or facts that might jog your memory. For example, the facts of a problem question might remind you of a particular case (examiners often base problem questions on similar facts to decided cases) or a particularly unusual word might trigger your recall.

- **Try something else.** If your mind goes blank on one question, and you are none the wiser after reading it again, then move on to another question. You can always come back to the first one you tried later on, but it is important not to stall on one question for too long.

- **Look to see if the topic is hidden.** It may be that your mind has gone blank because you were banking on a particular topic coming up but it does not appear to be on the paper. Look carefully at the other questions to see if the topic is hidden within another question. Examiners sometimes like to mix and match topics in order to test your ability to put material together. If you cannot find your dream topic, consider whether there are elements of it that you could introduce within another answer – but take care to ensure that its use is relevant and that you are not simply trying to answer the question that you wish had been asked (see Chapters 8 and 9 on techniques for essays and problem questions in exams).

- **Just write something.** Even if you have done nothing more than a bare modicum of revision, it is highly unlikely that you will find yourself in the exam room with absolutely nothing to say. However, if you find that you are unable to manage a whole question, then look for questions where you can at least offer some sort of answer. Remember that you only need to reach the pass mark.

Fear of failure and lack of perfection

The final category of student fears are concerned with the related issues of lack of perfection and fear of failure.

- **Be realistic.** You should retain a sense of your own ability. If your coursework marks were never higher than 52 per cent, it is probably unrealistic to expect that you will get 68 per cent in the exam. If you set unrealistic goals for yourself, you will most likely end up being disappointed. Aim to do your best and recognise that none of us can be perfect all of the time.

- **It is not coursework.** You should not expect your answer to be as polished as your coursework. It stands to reason that with time, research materials, a library and online resources, a piece of coursework will be more highly crafted than an exam answer. Examiners do realise this and make allowances accordingly.

- **It does not need to be immaculately presented.** In many ways, this is related to the previous point. Although exam answers have to be legible (see Chapter 7), do not become obsessed with neatness to the extent that it slows you down in the exam room.

- **It need not contain every case or statute.** It is not the end of the world if you are unable to remember a particular fact, case or provision. It is perfectly possible to achieve a first class mark with a minor omission. This is another reason why you should try to avoid the exam post-mortem. Although it is human nature to talk about how the exam went, there is nothing that you can do to change the outcome once you have put your pen down. The worst scenario is that fear of having done something awful in one exam puts even more pressure on you for the next.

- **You are doing it for yourself.** Some students are terrified of disappointing their parents, but this pressure is usually self-imposed, unrealistic or built up into something far greater than it actually is. If you are worried, then you should talk to your parents and explain how you are feeling. You might find that the level of pressure from them is not as great as you might have feared.

www.pearsoned.co.uk/lawexpress

■ To find out more ...

Visit the Companion Website where you will find a downloadable checklist of things to remember before the exam to ensure that you are prepared even if you are short of time.

NOTES

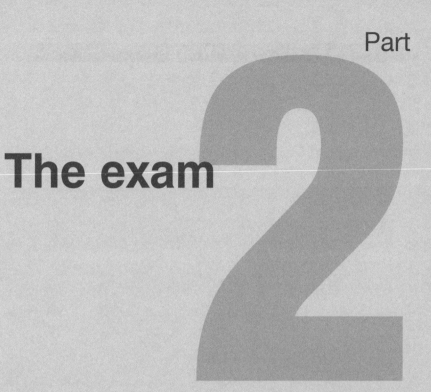

Part

The exam

Improving exam performance

7

Revision checklist

Topics covered in this chapter:

- [ ] Producing answers with accurate and relevant content
- [ ] Creating structured and focused answers that address the question
- [ ] Planning your answers
- [ ] Organising your time in the exam
- [ ] Effective use of statute books
- [ ] Producing legible answers

■ Introduction

The marks achieved in exams have a direct influence on the overall degree classification that students will receive at the end of their studies. As such, it is essential that you are able to perform to the best of your ability in exams so that you achieve marks that reflect your ability. Unfortunately, many students feel that they do not perform as well as they could and that there is a gap between the marks that they have the potential to achieve and the marks that they actually receive in exams. If you receive marks that are lower than you were hoping to achieve then, unless you have unrealistic expectations or a false sense of your ability, something must have gone wrong to limit the success of the answers that you produced in the exam. This chapter will help you to improve your exam performance by highlighting some of the factors that limit success in exams and by suggesting ways that these problems can be avoided or overcome, thus maximising your potential to achieve marks that reflect your hard work and ability.

■ Inadequate response to the question

The commonest problem that limits the marks awarded to an answer relates to its content. Examiners are looking for answers that are accurate, complete and contain only relevant points. Answers that contain errors, miss important points or are full of irrelevant detail will not receive good marks. There are a number of factors that contribute to the production of an answer that lacks sufficient accurate and relevant content.

Insufficient knowledge

If you do not have sufficient knowledge about a topic, it will be difficult to produce an answer that is accurate and provides a full response to the question. The consequence of insufficient knowledge is the production of an answer which has one of the following problems:

- **Too short.** Students who do not know enough about a topic often stop writing as soon as they run out of things to say and the result is a very short answer which is usually heavily descriptive. How short is too short? It is difficult to generalise as much depends on the size of the student's writing but, as a general rule, less than two sides of the booklet rings alarm bells with the examiner.

- **Filled out with waffle, repetition or irrelevance.** It is sometimes the case that students realise that they have not written a long enough answer so they fill up a few more pages by expanding on points that have already been made, by rewording the same points or by diverging into other areas of discussion. Although this produces a longer answer, it is unlikely to achieve any greater success.

- **Contains errors.** Most exam booklets contain one or two minor errors and these need not be fatal to the attainment of a solid overall mark. However, answers that contain one or two significant errors or many minor inaccuracies will not find favour with the examiner.

EXAM TIP

Test your knowledge before you start writing to make sure you know enough about the subject matter to answer the question. Brainstorm on a piece of rough paper and see how many points you can generate, noting the points you need to raise to describe the area of law and listing the arguments that you could make that are relevant to the question. As a rough rule of thumb, you should be able to make three separate arguments in order to provide a satisfactory essay.

Insufficient knowledge is likely to be the result of either lack of understanding of the area of law that is the subject matter of the question or a failure of memory.

Lack of understanding should not follow you into the exam room. In other words, be realistic when you are selecting topics to revise and eliminate any which you have not grasped. Do not fall into the trap of trying to memorise facts about a topic that you do not understand just because you think there will be a question on it. Examiners can recognise the difference between recall and understanding in the exam so you would be better off spending your revision time on topics that you have grasped.

STUDENT EXPERIENCE

I was in a panic because we'd been told that there would be at least two questions on negligence in our tort exam and just couldn't get my head round it. I went to see my tutor to see if he could help me but he just said 'well, even if there's three questions on negligence then there's still five questions left that you might be able to answer'. I revised all the syllabus except negligence and was easily able to answer four questions and I got a really good mark.

David

Exams do place a great deal of strain on your memory and it is possible that you may struggle to remember all the law that you have revised in the exam. There are a number of things that you can do to reduce the possibility that this will happen:

- Incorporate memory testing activities into your revision to practice and strengthen your powers of recall.

- Make sure you know enough about a question to attempt to answer it by jotting down a list of (relevant) points that you could include in your answer. If you cannot think of enough points at the planning stage, do not start writing in the hope that more material will occur to you as you are writing.

- Do not overstretch your memory by overloading it with unnecessary information. There is no need to learn case citations or to memorise the precise wording of quotations or other points that you want to remember.

- In particular, do not try to commit an entire answer to memory. Some students produce 'model' answers during the revision period and memorise them to write out in the exam. It is very unlikely that your answer will be a good response to the question and, as mentioned above, examiners can distinguish between memorisation and understanding.

- Use the techniques outlined in Chapter 5 to help you to commit material to memory and to trigger recall in the exam.

The most important point to bear in mind here is that things that you understand are easier to remember because they have passed into your long-term memory, so concentrate on developing knowledge during the revision period rather than committing a series of meaningless facts to memory.

EXAM TIP

Students worry about remembering the names of cases. If you cannot remember a case name in the exam, try to recall some other information about it that will identify it to the examiner:

- **Facts**: in the case where the defendant found a snail in a bottle of ginger beer.

- **Outcome**: in a case where the court ruled that damages would not be available for nervous shock to family members who heard about traumatic events indirectly by seeing news coverage on the television.

- **Judge**: in a case where Lord Bridge considered the relationship between European law and Parliamentary sovereignty.

Mismatch between question and answer

Your answer must be a perfect match to the question. Every question has parameters. In other words, an essay question is not simply about a particular topic but instead it asks you to discuss some specific point about that topic. Similarly, a problem question is designed to prompt an analysis of particular areas of law and not others. In order to create an answer that is a perfect match to the question, you must identify the focus of the question and select only material relevant for this focus for inclusion so that you make all the points that the question needs without discussing anything irrelevant.

Problems of this nature tend to arise either because students have misinterpreted the question or have disregarded it entirely.

Misinterpreting the question

The time constraints of the exam creates a pressured environment in which students tend to be eager to start writing as soon as possible. A hurried reading of a question that latches on to a key word or phrase contained in an essay title can lead to a misunderstanding of what the question requires. Problem questions contain even more potential for misinterpretation because they are usually long and often quite complicated as they are designed to test your skill at untangling the facts.

It is essential that you take the time to read the question carefully so that you are clear about what it requires. Failure to do this may lead to a situation in which you have produced a good answer, but to a different question than that which appears on the exam paper. If your answer does not address the question asked then it will achieve limited success. The following tips should help you to avoid this situation:

- Have a look at the section on time management that appears later in this chapter for guidance on planning your time in the exam. You will see that this includes allocating time for reading the exam paper and planning each answer.

- Get into the habit of dividing an essay question into its content words (which identify subject matter) and process words (which tell you what to do in relation to the content). You will find a discussion of this with examples in Chapter 8.

- In relation to problem questions, you must make sure that you adhere to the instructions at the end of the facts, as it is these that set the focus for your answer. You should also work through the facts carefully to identify the issues that need to be addressed. These points are covered in detail in Chapter 9.

Ignoring the question

Many students are so intent on capturing as much of the information about a topic that they have learned in the exam booklet that they overlook the requirements of the question completely. Having anticipated that a question will be asked on a particular topic, they have learned a series of points about that topic that they will include in their answer irrespective of what the question actually asks about it. This can lead to a very general answer that is far too abstract from the question.

Remember that an answer to an essay question should not just be a description of that topic but a discussion of something associated with that topic (see Chapter 8 for tips on achieving a balance between description and analysis in essay questions). In other words, each essay question takes a specific slant on a topic. This means that some of the things that you know about this topic will simply not be relevant to the particular question that has been asked about this topic, so to include them will actually weaken your answer.

EXAM TIP

Do not 'throw the kitchen sink' at your answers by writing every single thing you can remember about the essay topic. You will get more credit for shorter, more focused essays that demonstrate your ability to select only relevant points for inclusion than you will for a longer answer that tells the examiner everything that you know about a topic irrespective of its relevance to the specific question asked.

Of course, equipping yourself with some essential pieces of information that are likely to have a role in any question about a particular topic can be useful. The trick is to ensure that these are explained in the context of the question asked and to ensure that you tailor your material to suit the question.

Question spotting creates particular perils in relation to answers that ignore the question. This occurs when students have predicted that a particular question will be asked and have prepared an answer to it that they memorise and reproduce in the exam. This is never a good strategy. Not only is it highly unlikely that you will actually encounter the precise question that you have predicted, it is also the case that prepared and memorised answers are easily recognised by the examiner and will not attract great marks. This is because exams are designed to reward knowledge and understanding, not memory.

 Lecturer viewpoint

Answer the question that you have been asked, not the question that you wish you had been asked.

Insufficient legal skills

Students tend to be very knowledge-focused when it comes to exams. There is a widely held belief that marks are awarded for accurate knowledge irrespective of the way that it is used or presented. This is not correct. Your exam paper should not be an outpouring of legal knowledge, but a careful combination of knowledge and skills that produces the required number of organised, focused and well-argued answers.

Structure and organisation

Irrespective of whether you are writing an essay or answering a problem question, your answer should contain a logical line of argument. This means that it has to have a sensible starting point and that each of its points must fit together to create a cohesive response to the question. As many students, in the pressure of the exam room, simply start writing without any clear idea of where their answer is going, many exam answers are rather disorganised and jump about from point to point.

Lecturer viewpoint

Lack of planning is very visible in many exam answers. A lot of essays would get much better marks if the content was simply reorganised into a better structure: the same material in a different order would attract a lot more marks.

The way to achieve a well-structured answer is to take five minutes to make a plan of your answer before you start writing. Think about how the various points that you want to include will fit together and make a conscious decision about the order in which they will appear. The planning process should also help you to filter out irrelevant material.

Try this

Planning an answer

1 Start by reading the question paper thoroughly and making a note beside each question of the key words that reflect the content. Use this as a preliminary opportunity to highlight questions that you would like to answer and to eliminate those that do not seem attractive.

2 Select a question that you feel you could answer and make a list of the points that you could include. Make a realistic evaluation of whether the points that you have identified give you enough material to create a full answer.

3 Scrutinise your points with a critical eye to ensure that each point is relevant to the question. Remember that the inclusion of irrelevant points will not attract credit and may actually weaken your answer.

4 Group the points that you have listed together to create potential paragraphs and organise these in the order that you think they would flow most effectively. Do not be content with your first attempt at structure: you might find that switching points around creates a more powerful and persuasive argument. Remember that time spent making decisions about organisation now will save you time when you are writing your answer out.

The formulation of a plan of your answer should enable you to create an answer that captures all the points that you want to make. This should avoid the common problem, much disliked by examiners and a very clear sign of poor planning, of 'add in' paragraphs at the end of the answer with the note 'insert this at the top of the second page'.

Lack of analysis or application

It cannot be emphasised enough that it is not just what you know that is important in an exam but what you do with your knowledge. In essence, the most important attribute of an essay is its analysis of the law and the corresponding trait in an answer to a problem question is its application of the law to the facts.

An essay which merely describes the relevant law does not and cannot answer the question that was asked about the law. An essay requires a combination of description and analysis which means that you have to provide an outline of the relevant law that forms the foundation of the line of discussion that you then present. It is essential that your essay has a line of argument that tackles the specific issues raised by the question or it will simply be an abstract explanation of the law. Similarly, your task when answering a problem question is to use the law to predict the outcome of the hypothetical case presented in the facts.

Remember, you will not encounter any question on an exam paper at any point of your study of the law that requires nothing but a description of the law. Every question will ask you to do something with the law. A failure to do what is required will result in an answer that does not fulfil the requirements of the question.

> **STUDENT EXPERIENCE**
>
> When I moot, I write instructions to myself on cards and keep them on the table to act as reminders. I've started doing something similar in exams. As soon as the exam starts, I write things like 'make a line of argument' and 'apply the law to the facts' in a bright colour and really big letters on the question paper so that I see them every time I look at the question. I think it really helps me to remember what I'm supposed to be doing.
>
> *Dev*

There is a detailed breakdown of the process of writing analytical essays and applying the law to the facts in problem questions in Chapters 8 and 9 respectively.

Using authority

It should go without saying that your answer should include reference to legal authority such as statutory provisions and case law as well as, where appropriate, to secondary sources such as academic articles. However, you would be surprised to find that many exam answers do not contain a single reference to any of these sources. This is a significant limiting factor, so make sure that your answers incorporate references to law. The sections that follow set out some suggestions for using authorities effectively in your answers.

Statutes

One of the primary ways in which you should use the law in your answers is to indicate to the examiner where the legal rule that you are stating can be found. In other words, you should state the source of the law that you are using. This can be incorporated into your answer or added in brackets as a reference at the end of the relevant sentence.

Example: Incorporating statutory authority

■ Section 4 of the Trustee Act 2000 sets out the standard investment criteria that trustees must consider when making decisions about trust funds.

■ The standard investment criteria set out the factors that trustees must consider when making decisions about trust funds (section 4 of the Trustee Act 2000).

Exercise caution when quoting from statutes, especially if you have a statute book in the exam (see below) as there is little to be gained by long recitations of legislation. Be selective and extract the parts of the law that are needed to support your answer. As with everything else in your answers, let your argument determine your content rather than allowing your argument to be shaped by your content.

Case law

Case law may also provide a source of legal authority. If the area of law is governed by the common law rather than by statute, you should include reference to the key case or cases that set out the requirements of the law in the same way that you would if the matter were set out in statute.

Cases may also be used to elaborate on the meaning of statutory provisions. It is often the case that a statute sets out a framework of the law and case law then defines and refines its provisions through cases that are bought before the courts.

Example: Case law refining a statute

Section 4 of the Trustee Act 2000 sets out the standard investment criteria that trustees must take into account when making decisions about trust funds. This emphasises profitability and the spreading of risk when selecting investments. It is questionable whether trustees can select investments on the basis of the ethical views of trustees if this is likely to compromise profitability. In *Cowan* v. *Scargill*, a case predating the Trustee Act, the courts ruled that it was not permissible for trustees to select investments that reflected the ethical concerns of the trustees.

The final way in which case law can be used to good effect in your answers is to make use of their facts rather than their legal principle. In an essay, you could use the facts of a case to illustrate a point or by way of example. The facts of cases are particularly useful when answering problem questions. When you are deciding how the law should apply, you can use case law to support your preferred outcome. Remember, if you want to follow the outcome of the case, emphasise the similarities between its facts and those of the problem and highlight the differences if you want to reach a different conclusion.

You will find a detailed discussion of the use of case law in problem questions in Chapter 9.

Academic authority

The ability to refer to academic authority – that is, books and articles written by academics – can really make your answer stand out and impress the examiner. It demonstrates that you have read widely in preparation for the exam and the ideas that you encounter in these sources can provide great inspiration for critical arguments to present in an essay.

 Try this

Academic authority

If you are revising a topic in preparation for an essay question, then think about the most interesting or contentious points about that topic and see if you can find an article about it. You can do this by searching Westlaw, looking at the references provided in your textbook or consulting the suggested reading set out by your lecturer. When you have found an article, read through it and try to capture each main point that the author is making in a single sentence and make this part of your revision.

Do remember, though, that you should only incorporate these points into your answer if the question justifies it. There is always a temptation to want to include things that you have learned during your revision as it feels like a waste if you do not make use of it. However, you should always remember that your ultimate objective is to create effective answers that receive good marks and the inclusion of any irrelevant material will weaken your answer. It is true that the use of academic authority will impress the examiner, but only if it serves a purpose in your answer, otherwise it will look like you are including things just for the sake of it. Finally, you should remember to give clear information about the source of the information. You could write something like 'as Professor Jacobs argues in his article in the *Modern Law Review* in 2009 …' as this enables your examiner to authenticate your source.

Time management

In order to get a good overall mark in an exam, you must answer the correct number of questions and your answers must be complete and sufficiently detailed. This can be a problem when working within the time constraints of the exam, so the ability to manage the limited time available is an essential skill.

 Lecturer viewpoint

It is always disappointing to find that a student's final answer is limited to half a page of bullet points and a note that says 'out of time', particularly if the rest of the answers are strong. Obviously, you try to give as much credit as possible for what has been written but, at the end of the day, you can't award marks for things that haven't been written and it wouldn't be fair to students who have written four full answers to award a mark based upon what the student might have written if they had the time.

It is very difficult to obtain a good exam mark if you only answer three questions when four answers are required. In order to get 60 per cent overall in an exam, you have to produce four answers that are, in effect, worth 15 marks out of a possible 25. However, if you only answer three questions, each of these has to get 20 marks out of a possible 25 (which works out as 80 per cent each) in order for you to reach 60 per cent overall, which is a very tall order.

Make sure that you do not put yourself in this position by organising your time in the exam to ensure that you always attempt the correct number of questions.

 Try this

Calculating the time available per question

1   Start by dividing the duration of the exam by the number of questions you have to answer. For example, if you have to answer four questions in three hours, you have a maximum of 45 minutes available to answer each question.

2   Deduct five minutes to read the paper at the beginning and 15 minutes to check and edit your answers at the end of the exam. This reduces the maximum time available to 40 minutes for each question.

3   Allocate five minutes per question for planning your answer. You are left with a maximum of 35 minutes to answer each question.

▶

4 Create a time plan based upon these calculations. Highlight the time at which you expect to start working on each question, write these times in large print on a piece of scrap paper and keep it displayed prominently on your desk in the exam.

10 – 10.05	Read exam paper thoroughly.
10.05 – 10.10	Plan first answer.
10.10 – 10.45	Write first answer.
10.45 – 10.50	Plan second answer.
10.50 – 11.25	Write second answer.
11.25 – 11.30	Plan third answer.
11.30 – 12.05	Write third answer.
12.05 – 12.10	Plan final answer.
12.10 – 12.45	Write final answer.
12.45 – 1	Review and amend answers.

Once you have created a time plan for the exam, make sure that you stick to it. If you have not finished answering the first question at 10.45am, stop writing anyway and move on to the second question, leaving a few blank pages in your answer book so that you can come back and complete the first question at the end of the exam.

EXAM TIP

You will get more marks for attempting four questions in the exam, even if one or more of these is incomplete, than you will for producing three complete answers. If you realise that there is only ten minutes of the exam remaining, start to write your final answer rather than using the time to finish your third answer.

■ Using statute books

Many universities allow students to take statute books into the exam room. A statute book is a collection of all the legislation relevant to a particular subject within the law. There are several different statute books on the market produced by different publishers. They tend to be very much the same in terms of content but differ in the way that they organise the statutes in the book: alphabetically, chronologically or by theme.

The ability to take a statute book into the exam can be a real bonus as it relieves you of the pressure of having to memorise statutory provisions. However, there are some pitfalls associated with statute book use that you should know and take care to avoid.

If the regulations leave you free to make your own choice of statute book, take time to compare two or three from different publishers and think about which one you would find easiest to use in the exam. For example, if you struggle to remember the year that legislation was enacted, it might be easier to opt for alphabetical organisation in preference to chronological. Check also to see whether the book has an index as this can be helpful if you have forgotten the name of the statute that contains a particular provision.

Know the rules

Every university has its own regulations about the use of statute books in law exams. Make sure you know what the rules are at your own institution and follow them to the letter because your statute book will be checked in the exam and any breach will result in your book begin taken away by the exam invigilator.

Most universities do not permit the use of statute books which have been annotated so do not write in your statute book if you want to use it in the exam. Invigilators are notorious for their stringent application of the rules and may confiscate a statute book that has been annotated even if the annotations have been removed or obscured by crossing out, using correction fluid or rubbing out pencil notes. It has even been known for an invigilator to take away a statute book that had the student's name and address written at the front in case these were fictitious details that contained hints to help the student remember case names. The only way to be certain that your statute book will not fall foul of a prohibition on annotation is not to write in it at all.

There are other ways in which a statute book can be marked to make it easier to navigate in the exams but do check to see whether these are permitted at your university:

- Underlining or other (non-writing based) markings such as circling or asterisks to draw attention to key words or phrases.
- Highlighting key statutory provisions or words. You could use different colours for different purposes: for example, pink for section numbers and yellow for key phrases.
- Sticky tabs or Post-it notes can be used to mark the position in the book of statutes that you expect to use most often. Depending on the rules at your university, you may be able to write the name of the statute on the tab for ease of reference.

If the regulations at your university require a perfectly 'clean' book then you will not be permitted to highlight, underline or add tabs to your book. You may still be able to bend down the corners of relevant pages or mark up the book once you are in the exam room.

In our first year, we were allowed to highlight and use tabs before the exam, but the rules were changed in the second year so that we couldn't do this any more. I took my highlighters and sticky tabs into the exam with me and spent the first few minutes of the exam marking up my book. I think that this saved me time overall as it made it so much easier to find things. I also found that having something easy to do right at the start of the exam distracted me and stopped me feeling nervous.

Julianne

Use it effectively

You need to be able to find the law that you want quickly in the exam. To do this requires a solid grasp of the law itself and familiarity with the layout of the statute book.

Some students make the mistake of relying on the statute book as a source of knowledge. In other words, they do not have an understanding of the law prior to the exam but assume that they will simply be able to look it up in the statute book. This is not a good approach. The statute book is not there to teach you the law in the exam for the first time but to act as a quick reference guide so that you can ensure that you find the correct section numbers and can set out the requirements of the law with accuracy.

EXAM TIP

Learn the section numbers and general scope of important statutory provisions as part of your revision. Familiarise yourself with the layout of your statute book before the exam to ensure you can locate the provisions easily.

Quote from it sparingly

It is not a good use of time to copy statutory provisions out of the statute book into your exam booklet. Copying out something that has been provided for you does not demonstrate any knowledge and so has little potential to attract marks from the examiner. Many examiners find it quite annoying when they are confronted with lengthy quotations from statute.

 Lecturer viewpoint

Why do students write out chunks of statute in the exam? It is such a waste of time. They've got a statute book in front of them so why on earth would they think that we award marks for demonstrating an ability to copy from it?

It is possible that the reason that so many students write out the statutory provisions in full is because it feels like a good way of ensuring that there is accurate legal content in their answer. This often leads students to write out far more of the statute than is actually needed in the answer. Remember that content must be relevant as well as accurate in order to attract marks so if you do include a quotation from the statute in your answer, make sure that this is limited to the words that are absolutely necessary to your answer rather than copying long sections in their entirety. In fact, you will demonstrate more knowledge by extracting the phrase or sentence from the section that is of direct relevance to your answer than you will by copying out the entire section indiscriminately. Paraphrasing the requirements of a statutory provision can also demonstrate your understanding of the law by showing the examiner that you can express the requirements of the law in your own words with accuracy.

Example: Key phrases and paraphrasing

Full statutory provision

Section 6 of the Theft Act 1968 provides that 'a person appropriating property belonging to another without meaning the other permanently to lose the thing itself is nevertheless to be regarded as having the intention of permanently depriving the other of it if his intention is to treat the thing as his own to dispose of regardless of the other's rights; and a borrowing or lending of it may amount to so treating it if, but only if, the borrowing or lending is for a period and in circumstances making it equivalent to an outright taking or disposal'.

Use of a key phrase

According to section 6 of the Theft Act 1968, a person who borrows property may be considered as having an intention permanently to deprive if 'the borrowing ... is for a period and in circumstances making it equivalent to an outright taking or disposal'.

Paraphrasing

Under section 6 of the Theft Act 1968, a defendant who intends only to deprive a person of their property temporarily by borrowing it may nonetheless be regarded as having an intention permanently to deprive depending on the circumstances in which the property was borrowed.

■ Illegible writing

It would be unrealistic to expect students to fill exam booklets with their best handwriting. The time pressures of the exam and lack of practice at handwriting for hours at a time combine to explain why handwriting deteriorates as the exam progresses. However, you need to ensure that your writing does not become illegible so that the examiner cannot understand what you have written.

Lecturer viewpoint

My position on illegible writing is simple: if I can't read it, I don't mark it.

Approaches taken to illegible scripts vary. Some lecturers will just ignore anything that they cannot read, which means that you are not getting any credit for your work, whereas others will make a considerable effort to decipher illegible writing. Some universities make provision in their examination regulations for students to come in and dictate their answers or to pay for their exam booklets to be transcribed, which at least means that your work will be deciphered and marked. However, this is not necessarily an automatic right so do not assume that it will be offered to you.

STUDENT EXPERIENCE

When I failed European law, I asked to see my exam paper so that I could understand where I'd gone wrong. I was horrified to find that all but the first two-and-a-half pages had been crossed out in red with 'illegible' written in the margin. I knew my writing went a bit chaotic in exams but I'd always believed that we got the chance to have it typed up, but apparently this is at the examiner's discretion and he'd preferred just to cross out what he couldn't read. I was really gutted that I had to resit European law not because my answers weren't good but because my examiner couldn't read my writing.

Tom

The best course of action is to ensure that your writing does not become illegible. If you know that your writing becomes a scrawl under time constraints, you may need to accept that you will need to slow down and take more time to write in a way that can be read by the examiner. It is better to produce shorter answers that can be read, understood and given credit rather than more detailed answers that have sections that cannot be read by the examiner.

If you think that your writing may become illegible during the exams, try some of these tips to see if it makes a difference:

- **Experiment with different types of pen.** Some people believe that thicker pens put less pressure on the nerves in your arm so that your hand aches less and your writing stays relatively tidy. Switching between different types of pen in the exam might also be helpful as it alters the position of the muscles.

- **Practise writing for long periods of time.** The muscles in your hand are not used to writing for three-hour stretches. Like any other muscles, these will strengthen with practice so use the revision period to build up your ability to write for long periods of time without interruption.

■ **Modify your writing style in the exam.** Small letters, sloping writing and closely spaced words are harder for others to read so try to adapt your writing style to create larger upright letters that are easy to read. Writing on every other line of the exam booklet can be a useful way of achieving this. Some students resort to printing their answers in capital letters towards the end of the exam as their writing deteriorates.

Follow the rubric

The rubric is the set of instructions that govern the way that the exam paper should be tackled. It is important that you read the instructions and comply with their stipulations. Some contraventions will result in a loss of marks – for example, if you fail to answer the correct number of questions – whereas others will not result in a direct loss of marks but may annoy your examiner (and it is not a good idea to annoy the person who is responsible for awarding marks to your answers).

Answer the correct number of questions

Check carefully to make sure you know how many questions need to be answered. There is no credit to be gained by tackling more than the required number of questions as the examiners will simply ignore the additional answers.

STUDENT EXPERIENCE

I was talking to one of my friends after the medical law exam and we were swapping notes about what questions we had answered. She had answered four questions and I'd only answered three so I was in a real panic in case I hadn't answered enough questions but, luckily for me, it was her mistake as she'd assumed it was four questions because that was what we had in all our other exams.

Emily

A failure to answer enough questions will have an obvious impact on the marks that can be awarded to your paper.

Answer particular questions

The exam paper might contain instructions that govern your choice of questions. For example, there might be a compulsory question or the paper might be divided into two parts with an instruction that you must answer at least one question from each part. Again, failure to follow the instructions will have a detrimental impact on your marks as credit cannot be given for answers that are not in compliance with the rubric. For example, if you have to answer three questions with at least one from Part A and one from Part B, this means that the maximum number of questions that you can answer from Part A is two (because at least one question from Part B must be answered). If you answer three questions from Part A, only the first two will be marked, the third one will be ignored and a mark of zero will be awarded for the missing answer from Part B.

The front of the answer book

The front of the answer book has a number of sections that you will need to complete, so make sure that you provide all the necessary information. This will include your name and student number as well as writing the number of exam booklets that you have used and listing the numbers of the questions that you have answered.

 Lecturer viewpoint

Students who don't write the question numbers on the front of the exam booklet really irk me, because it means that I have to do it and it is surprising how much time it takes up when you've got a hundred papers to mark. When I see an exam booklet with no question numbers on the front, I feel grumpy with the student before I've even read a single word that they've written!

Inside the answer book

Two instructions that are common to every university and which are routinely ignored by quite a few students are that you should not write in the margins and that you should start every answer on a fresh page. These requirements are designed to ensure that your examiners have room to record their thoughts as they work through your answers and to summarise their impression of your answer at the end. If you do not leave them room to write, there is a risk that the examiner will forget some of the good points about your answer when deciding what mark to award, so it is important to adhere to these rules.

www.pearsoned.co.uk/lawexpress

■ To find out more ...

Visit the Companion Website where you will find some sample answers to exam questions. Use your understanding of the law and your knowledge of common weaknesses in exam answers gained from this chapter to identify the problems with the answers and see if you can put them right.

NOTES

Writing essays in exams

8

Revision checklist

Topics covered in this chapter:

- [ ] Understanding the requirements of an essay question
- [ ] Analysing the question
- [ ] Creating an essay plan
- [ ] Writing an essay in exam conditions
- [ ] Incorporating authority into an essay
- [ ] Common faults and how to avoid them

■ Introduction

Writing an essay in exam conditions presents challenges that do not exist in relation to the production of a coursework essay. The time constraints of the exam combined with the need to remember all the relevant legal principles, arguments and cases creates pressure to 'get words on paper' as quickly as possible. Whilst it may be comforting to fill the exam booklet with words, this does not necessarily produce an effective essay. Indeed, most lecturers are agreed that the commonest problem that limits the success of essays written in exams is that they do not answer the question but are instead an outpouring of everything that the student can remember about the topic irrespective of its relevance to the question. This chapter will help students to create more effective essays by providing a step-by-step guide to analysing the question, selecting relevant material and creating a plan that leads to the production of a focused and flowing essay that answers the question that has been set.

■ Impress the examiner

The starting point for this chapter is to consider what characteristics an essay produced in exam conditions should have in order to impress the examiner.

- **Relevant and accurate content.** The acid test of relevance is whether the content is necessary to answer the particular question asked, not whether the content touches on the general topic of the question. This tests your ability to identify the focus of the question and respond by selecting relevant material for inclusion in your essay. Accuracy is concerned with the correctness and completeness of the content of the essay thus tests your ability to recall the law that you have learned.

- **An appropriate balance between description and analysis.** A good essay is a combination of description of a particular legal topic and discussion which answers a specific question about that topic. Excessive description is one of the common weaknesses of essays produced in exams, so aim to include greater analysis in your answers in order to improve your marks.

- **Essay writing craftsmanship.** An essay requires a strong structure and a clear line of argument that develops as the essay progresses. It should start with an introduction and end with a conclusion that ties together the strands of arguments presented to provide a direct answer to the question. These skills are often abandoned in the exam room as students concentrate on capturing information on paper. This is unfortunate as the exam is designed to test not only what you know about the law but also your ability to communicate that knowledge effectively.

■ **Inclusion of authority.** Examiners like to see authorities such as statute, case law and articles used in essay questions. To do this requires wide reading, identification of the relevant material and the ability to recall the points made in these authorities in the exam. It also tests your ability to use authorities effectively in your essay; in other words, to use sources to develop your argument and to demonstrate your understanding, rather than simply mentioning them in passing or putting case names in brackets at the end of a sentence.

If you give some thought to these characteristics, you should realise that exams do not exist with the sole purpose of testing your memory. Exams aim to test knowledge, not memory. It is not enough to memorise a series of facts and cases and write them down in the exam booklet. Examiners encounter far too many essays that can be described as 'everything the student knows about x' and these answers achieve limited success because they do not do enough to demonstrate the knowledge and skills that the question was written to test.

A good essay that will impress the examiner is one that is a combination of knowledge, demonstrated by the careful selection of relevant points and authorities, and essay writing skills that use this material to create and develop a line of argument that provides a direct response to the question asked. Try to remember that it is not just what you know but how you use that knowledge that will lead to success in exams. This chapter will help you to develop the skills necessary to use your knowledge to produce a focused and analytical essay that will impress the examiners and be rewarded with good marks.

■ Answer the question

The most important piece of advice that you will be given is that you should answer the question. However, it may be the case that students do not really understand what lecturers mean by this advice. Perhaps the following experience sounds familiar.

STUDENT EXPERIENCE

I was really disappointed with my first year exam results. The marks were a lot worse than I'd expected but I knew that I'd worked really hard. I went to see my personal tutor and asked her for advice and she said 'you need to answer the question'. I was confused because I knew that I had answered the questions – I'd answered four questions on each paper and written about six pages for each answer. My personal tutor said that this wasn't what she meant and that I'd talked about the topics for six pages but that I hadn't answered the question but I don't really know what she means.

Will

Will's experience is an example of a common misunderstanding about what students and lecturers mean when they talk about answering a question. Will thinks he answered the question because he wrote several pages about the subject matter of the question. Will's lecturer thinks that he did not answer the question because he was writing about the topic in general terms rather than providing a targeted answer to the specific question that was asked about that topic.

If you are struggling to understand the difference, try thinking about what it means to answer a question in a context other than a law exam. Imagine that you have asked a friend how to make a pizza and they respond by outlining the history of pizza making, by telling you where you can buy a pizza and by explaining why they believe that pepperoni pizzas are better than ham and mushroom pizzas. They have provided a response to your question and it is on the right subject matter because they are talking about pizza but they have not answered your question. You know a lot of things about pizza that you did not want to know but you still do not know how to make a pizza. As such, their response to your question is of very little value. This is exactly the problem that often occurs in essays written in exams: students write about the general topic of the question or, worse still, answer the question that they wish they had been asked. However, if your essay does not tell the examiner the particular things that they wanted to know, it will achieve limited success.

The problem often arises because students store a great deal of information about law during the revision period and are anxious to get credit for it in the exam. It can be very frustrating if questions do not appear that enable you to use that knowledge that you have taken such pains to acquire. However, it is of vital importance that you appreciate that writing facts that you know about a topic that are not raised by the question will not gain any credit from the examiner; in fact, it may have the opposite effect and you will lose marks for including irrelevant material because it is not an accurate response to the question, as this example illustrates.

 Lecturer viewpoint

Recently, I marked an exam paper that included an essay on constructive manslaughter. The first two pages were quite good if a little descriptive – they set out the elements of the offence and identified one of the problems with it. Then the essay went off point into four pages of discussion of corporate manslaughter and gross negligence manslaughter, neither of which had any relevance to the question. If the essay had just stopped after the first two pages, I would've given it 56 but by the end of the two pages of irrelevant discussion the final mark that I gave the essay was 44.

The message here is clear: two pages of focused discussion that provides a direct answer to the question asked will achieve greater success than six pages of general discussion of the topic. Therefore, the key to greater success with essays written in exams is to avoid an outpouring of all knowledge of the topic in favour of careful selection of particular aspects of knowledge that are of direct relevance to the question. The process of achieving a focused answer is covered in the next sections of this chapter:

- Analysing the question to ascertain its precise requirements.

- Creating a plan that identifies the most relevant material for inclusion.

- Writing an essay in a way that emphasises the links between the material included and the question asked.

Analysing the question

The crucial first step in producing an effective essay that will impress your examiner is an analysis of the question to determine what it requires. Essay questions may be worded in a number of different ways but they all, in essence, require the same thing: firstly, a description of a particular area of law that is the topic of the essay and, secondly, some sort of discussion as to the nature, operation and effectiveness of that area of law.

Types of essay question

In order to identify what it is that needs to be described and what it is that needs to be discussed, you will need to unpick the essay title. Different types of question vary as to the extent of the guidance that they provide about what is required as the example which follows demonstrates.

Example: Different styles of essay questions

All three questions focus on the same subject matter – the *Ghosh* test of dishonesty in criminal law – but differ in the way that they communicate their requirements to the student.

1 Detailed instructions

Provide a brief outline of the *Ghosh* test and explain its role in the criminal law. Identify the criticisms that have been made of the *Ghosh* test and consider whether it is an effective means of establishing dishonesty.

2 Partial instructions

Critically assess whether the *Ghosh* test should continue to be used as the test of dishonesty in theft and other property-related offences.

3 Quotation questions

'The *Ghosh* test is too blunt an instrument to dissect the state of mind of the defendant. All pretence at insight into the defendant's mind should be abandoned in favour of a straightforward objective standard of dishonesty.'

Discuss this quotation.

The first question in the example above breaks the essay down into a series of points to be addressed. This provides a clear indication of what is required both in terms of description and discussion. By contrast, the second question identifies only the issue for discussion but it is implicit within this that sufficient description is needed to provide a setting within which that discussion can take place. In essence, this would involve inserting the first line of the first question into the second question. It is often the case that essay questions only stipulate the topic for discussion and it is assumed that the student will be able to identify what area of law needs to be described in order for that discussion to make sense.

The third question requires a discussion of a quotation. This is a popular method of presenting an essay and it is somewhat more challenging for the student as it requires the student to identify both the 'describe' and 'discuss' aspects of the question for themselves. Read the quotation carefully, identify the argument that it makes and consider this in light of the instruction that accompanies the quotation. Here, you are simply asked to discuss the quotation so it would be sensible to assume that you will need to describe the nature and function of the Ghosh test before entering into a discussion that explores whether the sentiment expressed in the quotation is correct.

Irrespective of how an essay is worded, remember to break it down into what needs to be described and what needs to be discussed and then make sure that you address both parts of the question. Remember that you cannot discuss the law until you have described it, but also that excessive description is one of the most common weaknesses of essay questions produced by students in exam conditions.

 Lecturer viewpoint

One of the greatest flaws in essays written in exams is excessive description. I read some essays that are exclusively descriptive with no attempt at analysis whatsoever and this really limits the marks that can be awarded. If I could give one piece of advice to students writing essays in an exam it would be that they should remember that every essay asks a question and that questions cannot be answered with description.

Content words and process words

One method that can be used to determine what aspects of an essay need to be described and what requires analysis is to identify the content words and process words in the essay question. An essay question is a combination of content words and process words. Content words identify the subject matter of the essay and process words tell the student what it is that must be done with that content.

The approach of analysing an essay question by reference to content and process words is known as the 'DO something TO something' approach. In other words, the process words tell you what to DO and the content words tell you what it is that must have something done TO it. This approach is demonstrated below:

Example: Content words and process words

Outline the aims of the Land Registration Act 2002 and determine whether the courts have interpreted its requirements so as to achieve these aims.

PROCESS WORDS: outline, assess

CONTENT WORDS: aims, Land Registration Act 2002, interpretation by the courts

From this, the 'DO what TO what' approach can be applied to establish the relationship between the process and content words:

- Outline the aims of the Land Registration Act 2002

- Determine how the courts have interpreted the Act

- Determine whether this interpretation is in line with the aims of the Act.

This gives you a clear picture of what the question requires and helps you to appreciate the way in which the question breaks down into description and discussion. The table below identifies some of the common process words used to formulate essay questions in law and divides them according to whether they indicate that description or discussion is required.

Process word	Meaning	Type
Analyse	Examine in close detail; break down into constituent parts; identify key points and show how they interrelate.	Discussion
Assess/critically assess	Consider the value or importance; weigh up; give both positive and negative viewpoints.	Discussion
Comment upon	A combination of 'analyse' and 'assess'; give a breakdown of the key points and consider their relative importance.	Discussion
Compare	Show similarities and differences between two points. Often conjoined with 'contrast'.	Discussion
Contrast	Show differences between two points and consider whether those differences are significant.	Discussion
Criticise	Consider arguments in favour of and against a proposition and reach a conclusion based on evidence, theories or assertions.	Discussion

▶

Define	Give the meaning of (in some cases there may be more that one meaning, so you may need to consider different possible definitions).	Description
Describe	Give a detailed description of the main points.	Description
Discuss	Outline key issues and evaluate the different arguments or points of view, based on evidence, theory or opinion. Evaluate the different points of view. Note that 'discuss' quotations are often deliberately provocative.	Discussion
Distinguish	Explain the differences between.	Discussion
Evaluate	Similar to 'discuss' but also requires a focus on the value or importance of an argument or point.	Discussion
Examine	Consider the subject in great detail. Often combined with 'assess' or 'evaluate'.	Discussion
Explain	Give details about how and why a particular point is so. Will generally combine both description (how) and discussion (why).	Description Discussion
Explore	Investigate different strands of arguments to determine whether a stated position is correct or can be established.	Discussion
Illustrate	Make clear by use of examples.	Discussion
Justify	Give reasons in favour of a particular position while considering possible alternative arguments against.	Discussion
Outline	Give a summary of the main points.	Description
State	Give a clear and brief presentation of.	Description
Summarise	Provide the key points only, without unnecessary detail or example.	Description
To what extent/ How far	Consider how true a proposition is, or its contribution towards a particular outcome. Such questions are usually not clear cut (the answer is seldom 'totally' or 'not in the slightest').	Discussion

▮ Planning your essay

Once you have analysed the question, you should have a clear idea of what it requires. You know what it requires you to describe and what line of argument is required in the discussion element of the essay. You will now be able to create a plan for your essay. The purpose of an essay plan is for you to make decisions about what material you will include in your essay, how you will group it together and how you will order the points that make up your argument.

Sadly, many students admit that they do not make a plan but just start writing their essay without any clear idea of where it is going and what line of argument they want to develop. This tends to lead to a rather disorganised essay in which the points do not flow in a logical order. Lack of planning also creates a risk that important points will be omitted. Remember, when you produce an essay using a computer, you can reorder the paragraphs at the click of a mouse and insert new material that has been forgotten but this is not possible with a handwritten essay. As a result, students who do not plan their essay before they start writing can get into terrible difficulties with their attempts to reorder their work and this does not find favour with examiners, as the following example highlights.

 Lecturer viewpoint

My pet hate is jigsaw essays. This is what I call essays where the students seem to have written the points in any order that occurs to them and then create a system of asterisks, arrows and notes saying 'insert this here' to tell me how the different paragraphs fit together. Not only are jigsaw essays annoying because they are hard to read and understand, they also give a very negative message that what I am reading is not the product of planning and organisation. I always think that a muddled essay is the sign of a muddled student.

The most common reason that students give for failure to create an essay plan is that it is a waste of the limited time available in the exam. It is true that time is short in the exam, but it is a mistake to think that taking five minutes per question to create a plan is time wasted. After all, in a three-hour exam with four questions, there is 45 minutes available to produce each answer. If you take five minutes to create a plan, you still have 40 minutes left to write your essay and you will not have to stop and think 'What do I write next?' because this decision will already have been made at the planning stage. Moreover, the end result is likely to be a better essay because you will taken time to make decisions about the order of points and the flow of your argument.

Lecturer viewpoint

Unplanned essays ramble. Time and time again, I encounter long and detailed essays that just ramble without any point and with little attempt to answer the question. Students really do need to understand that a shorter, more organised, essay that addresses the point raised by the question will get significantly more marks than a much longer and more detailed ramble. The important thing for students to remember is that marks are awarded for the quality of their essays, not the quantity of words written.

The point made here is an important one and it relates back to what lecturers are looking for in your essays. A free flow of consciousness that captures everything that you know about a topic is not impressive to the examiner. Remember that the purpose of the exam is to test your skills as well as your knowledge, so think about the skills involved in creating a successful essay by:

- Identifying the issues at the heart of the question.
- Selecting relevant material to enable those issues to be explored.
- Organising material so that a logical argument develops.
- Balancing competing arguments against each other.
- Including examples and authorities to support arguments made.
- Ensuring that each paragraph makes a contribution towards answering the question.

It will be easier to ensure that your essay has these characteristics if you spend time creating a plan so that you make conscious decisions about how your points fit together into an argument and how these combine to answer the question.

Try this

Essay planning

Follow these steps to create a preliminary plan for your essay that helps you to eliminate irrelevant material and to construct a logical argument that answers the question.

1. Looking at the broad topic of the essay, make a quick list of points that you could possibly consider. Do not worry about the order or their relevance at this stage; just get all your ideas down on paper.

2. Using your analysis of the question as a guide, test each of the points that you have listed for relevance to the question. Put a tick by points that are of direct

and obvious relevance and cross out those that are not relevant (remember that you are testing for relevance to the particular question and not to the broad topic). Look at the points that remain and try to reach a decision one way or another as to whether they need to be included. Remember that irrelevant material creates an inaccurate answer, so be ruthless.

3   Look at the points that remain and try to group them together. Try to identify at least three arguments that you are going to make in relation to the question asked and think about how these relate to each other.

4   You should now be able to make a preliminary list of paragraphs. Remember to start with description as this gives your discussion a foundation. Move on to discussion and ensure that each paragraph contains a single argument. Capture this in a sentence and support this with a list of key words and phrases that remind you of the points that you want to make.

5   Now check that every paragraph contains a central point that is relevant to the question. Consider also how each paragraph relates to the one that precedes it and scribble down words that make this relationship clear such as 'a second argument in favour' or 'a contrasting view'. This will remind you of how your argument fits together.

You will find a worked example of this approach on the Companion Website that shows each stage of the process.

Writing your essay

If you have taken the time to produce a plan which sets out the order of your points and the direction of your line of argument, it should be relatively straightforward to convert this into an essay. There are, however, still a couple of points to remember that are important to producing a good quality essay.

Introduction and conclusion

It should go without saying that your essay should have an introduction and a conclusion but, unfortunately, these are often missing from essays produced in exam conditions. This is an unfortunate omission as the introduction and conclusion play vital roles in creating the focus of your essay. The introduction unpicks the question and sets out for the examiner how you are going to approach it and what your line of argument will be, whereas the conclusion ties together all the strands of your argument into a single and direct response to the question. From a pragmatic point of view, the introduction is the first thing that your marker reads, so it gives them an initial impression of the quality of your work, so you want it to be a good one. Likewise, the conclusion is the final part of your essay that the examiner reads just before they decide what mark to award that answer, so it stands to reason that you want to leave them with a good impression of your work.

Paragraphing

Try not to abandon paragraphs altogether when writing by hand in your exam booklet. It is very daunting for a marker to face pages of unbroken writing. Remember that each paragraph should contain a single idea that builds on the previous paragraph and leads into the following paragraph. Students sometimes question how they can make decisions about paragraph content in an exam setting where it is not possible to amend or reword what has been written. The following approach is commonly used to assist in paragraph construction: it is based upon the statement of a single idea, its description, an example and a conclusion.

Idea	This states the subject matter of the paragraph. It should also indicate how the subject matter fits within the overall picture of the essay.	The second argument against expansive approach to the imposition of liability on public servants such as the police is the floodgates argument.
Explanation	This describes or defines the subject matter.	The crux of this is that to allow one case to succeed is undesirable, even if the case is clearly meritorious, because it will create a precedent that allows other similar claims to be brought before the courts.
Example	This offers some illustration of the principle in operation or offers an authority to develop the argument.	For example, it was held in *Stevens* v. *Thames Valley Police* that once a duty had been imposed on the police to prevent a crime from occurring, every offence that was committed could lead to a tortious claim against the police. Harris J suggested that this could lead to a claim by a man whose car had been stolen against the police who failed to arrest all the car thieves in the area.
Conclusion	This relates the point made back to the question or creates a link to the next paragraph.	Of course, this is an extreme example and it goes way beyond the suggestion that the police should have liability for a failure to protect identifiable victims from foreseeable harm as the question suggests.

Signposting

In an essay, you are presenting a line of argument. This means that it is important that the various points and paragraphs link together in a way that makes sense to the reader. When you are writing them, you already understand the relationship, but you need to ensure that you use signposting to make these relationships clear to the examiner. Signposting words and phrases are used to indicate to the reader the relationship between each point and between a point and the question. For example:

- In order to do x, it is first necessary to do y.

- Having done x, it is now possible to do y.

- There are three arguments to be considered.

- The first consideration is ...

- A second objection to this is ...

- A final point to discuss is ...

- Words which indicate that one argument build on and supports the previous point: moreover, in addition, furthermore.

- Words that indicate that a contrary opinion is about to be expressed which departs from the previous argument: however, conversely, an alternative view, by contrast.

■ Incorporating authority

Students often ask whether they should incorporate authority into their exam answers and, if so, how many authorities should be used in each question. The answer to the first question is 'yes, definitely', but it is impossible to provide a numerical response to the second question so the vague response 'as many as you need to support your answer' will have to suffice. In the sections that follow, the different types of authority and the way that they should be used in essay questions will be explained.

Primary authority

A primary authority is a source of law such as a statute or case. Every time that you state the law, you should include a reference to the primary authority that contains that legal principle. In other words, the purpose of a primary authority is to inform the reader of your work where the law that you have stated can be found.

When writing an essay in an exam, you should strive to include references to statutory provisions and cases that are the source of the law that you are discussing. For example, if you were discussing a statute-based topic such as theft, you would need to be able to reference the definition of theft found in section 1 of the Theft Act 1968 as well as the elaboration on the meanings of the five elements of theft found in section 2–6. In addition to this, you would be expected to make reference to leading cases which explained the interpretation or operation of these statutory provisions. If you were dealing with a topic that is part of the common law, such as negligence, your primary authorities would be the case law that establishes the principles of negligence and demonstrate its operation.

Identifying and committing to memory the relevant statutory provisions and leading case law in relation to each topic that you learn for the exam should be a central part of the revision process. You will find some useful hints and tips to help you to memorise authorities in Chapter 5.

What are leading cases?

The study of the law involves a great deal of case law and it would not be realistic to expect students to learn and remember all of them. For that reason, it is important that you are able to identify the leading cases to ensure that they are at the forefront of your revision.

A leading case is one which is considered as being particularly significant because it has progressed the law in some way and has become the primary point of reference for a legal principle or for the interpretation of a particular word or phrase; for example, *Donoghue* v. *Stevenson* [1932] AC 562 is a leading case because it established the neighbour principle at the heart of the tort of negligence and the later case of *Caparo* v. *Dickman* [1990] 2 AC 605 is also regarded as a leading case as it refined this principle, establishing the criteria that must be satisfied if negligence is to be established.

Most House of Lords (now Supreme Court) cases will be leading cases as an appeal cannot reach this highest level of court unless it raises a point of public importance. However, this does not mean that the lower courts cannot produce leading cases: for example, the test of dishonesty in theft was established by the Court of Appeal in *R* v. *Ghosh* [1982] QB 1053.

It may also be that a case is considered to be significant because it is only one that demonstrates a particular point of interest or importance. For example, *Elliot* v. *C* [1983] 1 WLR 939 might well be regarded as a leading case, although it was only decided in the Divisional Court and did not develop any new legal principle, simply because its facts provide such a striking illustration of the harshness of operation of the law that existed at the time.

If you are unsure whether a case is a leading case, consider how prominent it is by looking to see how much attention is given to it in textbooks and consider how much time was spent on it in lectures. You might also want to use resources such as the *Law Express* revision series which identify the leading cases and set out their facts and principles.

Secondary authority

Secondary authorities are explanations or discussions of the law such as those found in textbooks, monographs and articles. In essence, a secondary authority is someone's opinion on the law. These sources can be very useful as they help you to understand the law and may provide inspiration for points that are relevant to the discussion element of an essay question, such as pointing out criticisms that can be made of the law or highlighting areas where reform is needed. Moreover, the incorporation of secondary sources into your essay enables you to demonstrate that you have read widely about the topic and this is likely to impress the examiners far more than an account that follows the order of points made in the set textbook or which were presented in the lecture.

STUDENT EXPERIENCE

I was a bit sceptical when one of my lecturers suggested reading articles as part of our revision because it seemed like a lot of extra work that I hadn't done before and I was doubtful that I'd be able to remember anything from them. I picked three articles for each topic and tried to remember three key points from them and I can't believe what a difference it made. I felt far more confident at tackling essay questions because I felt that I actually had some sensible points to make in argument and also because it really boosted my confidence to be able to write things like 'writing in the *Criminal Law Review* in 2006, Professor Dennis criticised this decision because ...'. I just felt far more knowledgeable about the topics than I had in previous exams and my marks were much better. I usually get marks in the mid-50s for my exams but I was up in the mid-60s once I started using articles.

Eloise

■ Common problems

In this final section of the chapter, the focus will be on the problems that often arise in essay questions in exams with suggestions on how to avoid them.

Running out of steam

Some answers only span less than a single side of A4. Even worse, some exam booklets contain essays that are started and then crossed out so that a different question can be attempted. The problem here is that students have started writing a question before appreciating that they do not know enough about the subject matter to produce a complete essay. Avoid this problem by taking time to analyse the question and produce a plan so that you only start to answer questions if you are confident that you can produce a full answer.

Too much description

It is far easier to describe the law than it is to analyse it, so it is often the case that students, in the pressured setting of the exam room, fill their exam booklet with pages of description. This is not a good technique because all essays require discussion as well as description, so an essay that is purely or largely descriptive is limited in the success that it can achieve. Avoid excessive description by ensuring that you have some discursive points to make before deciding to attempt an essay. If you cannot identify three arguments that you could make that are relevant to the question (after you have analysed its requirements) then you should not really attempt it.

Irrelevant material

Without a clear idea of what the question requires, students may introduce irrelevant material into their essay. This tends to lead to the creation of an 'everything I know about x' essay in which the student writes everything that they can think of about the topic in a desperate attempt to get words on paper. Again, analysis of the question and the creation of an essay plan should help you to avoid this problem. Moreover, if you try to get into the habit of creating an explicit link between each paragraph and the question asked, this should help to strengthen your focus and enable you to eliminate irrelevant material.

Producing model answers

Model answers are loved by students and hated by examiners. A model answer is a 'perfect' answer created during the revision period to a question that is predicted to appear on the exam paper. The answer is memorised so that it can be reproduced in the exam. However, unless the student has made an uncannily accurate prediction, it is highly unlikely that the exact question anticipated will appear. Undaunted, some students simply produce their model answer as a response to a question on the same subject matter and this will meet with very little success as it is, quite simply, an answer to a different question. The easiest way to avoid this situation is not to prepare model answers in the first place. It is a far more effective use of your revision time to accumulate broad knowledge and to test this by writing practice answers to past questions in simulated exam conditions.

Answering only part of the question

If an essay question requires that you discuss the impact on a defendant's right to a fair trial of both anonymity orders and prohibitions on questioning regarding previous sexual history evidence, you should not tackle the question unless you can address both of the issues stipulated in the question. This can be frustrating if you have a very good knowledge of one of the issues, but to go ahead and tackle the question would be unwise as you know that you can only deal with half of it so you are restricting your ability to gain the marks that are available. Try to ensure that you are not in a position in which you can only answer half of a question by revising as much of the syllabus as possible. If necessity forces you to tackle such a question, do at least have an attempt at both parts; you might be surprised at how much knowledge floods back to you about an unrevised topic once you start to write about it.

Lack of legal argument

One of the sure signs of lack of knowledge is an answer that takes a very general line of argument that is lacking in legal content. In other words, the essay is one that an intelligent layperson who had never studied law could have produced. This tends to stem from lack of preparation, so the obvious solution is to ensure that sufficient revision is undertaken to enable a properly legalistic answer to be written, but it is sometimes the case that students are tempted into this sort of journalistic approach when they encounter topics on which there are well-known public opinions such as civil partnerships, continued membership of the European Union or the abolition of fox-hunting.

 Try this

Creating an essay plan

As you will have gathered from the emphasis placed on it in this chapter, the pre-writing stages of analysing the question and planning your answer are the key to success when producing successful essays in exam conditions. Using the methods outlined in this chapter, analyse the title of one of the following essays and create a plan of your answer. It would be a good idea to pick one that covers a topic that you have revised for a forthcoming exam or a topic that you are otherwise familiar with, such as one that has been the focus of a recent piece of coursework.

Criminal Law

The Corporate Manslaughter and Homicide Act 2008 was introduced to remedy the perceived inability of the common law offence of gross negligence manslaughter to impose criminal liability on organisations whose actions or inactions brought about the death of a blameless individual. Summarise the differences between the statutory approach and the common law offence and evaluate the extent to which, if at all, the former overcomes the limitations of the latter.

Contract

'After a few false starts, the courts have now developed a clear test of economic duress that offers a satisfactory resolution in cases where improper pressure has been applied.'

Outline the development of the law of economic duress and comment upon whether the statement is an accurate reflection of the state of the current law.

Land Law

Explain how an easement may be created by implicated and critically assess whether the grant of such easements amounts to an unreasonable interference with the property rights of the owner of land over which the easement exists.

Trusts

Outline the remedies that are available for breach of trust. Critically assess the extent to which these provide adequate protection of the beneficiary's interests.

European Law

Critically assess the effectiveness of the powers of enforcement available to the European Commission and the extent to which they are able to compel Member States to comply with European law.

Tort

Pure economic loss is treated differently from other forms of loss arising in tort. Explain the nature of economic loss and the circumstances under which it is recoverable in tort. Consider why it is treated differently and assess whether this distinction is justifiable.

Constitutional Law

'It is now judicially recognised that prerogative power is as capable of abuse as any other power.' (Wade and Forsyth)

Explain what is meant by prerogative powers and explore the extent to which the courts are able to regulate the exercise of prerogative powers.

www.pearsoned.co.uk/lawexpress

 To find out more . . .

Visit the Companion Website where you will find some essay plans that were produced by students in exams to the questions above. You can compare these with your plans to get ideas of how the questions could have been approached differently. You can also evaluate the plans on the basis of how effective you think they were in preparing the student to write a full essay that addressed the question.

NOTES

Answering problem questions in exams

Introduction

Problem solving is one of the core skills that is tested in the exams. Most exam papers – with the exception of very theoretical modules such as jurisprudence – contain a mix of essays and problem questions so it is important that you are able to tackle both types of question with equal amounts of confidence. The greatest challenge presented by problem questions in an exam is the necessity to untangle the complicated facts that are provided to ensure that you have a clear idea of who has done what to whom and how this may give rise to legal liability. This chapter will help you to develop an effective strategy for problem solving by sifting through the mass of information provided in the problem scenario and create a clear and organised answer that demonstrates your ability to apply the law to the facts and reach a reasoned conclusion about liability.

Impress the examiner

The starting point for this chapter is to consider what characteristics an answer to a problem question produced in exam conditions should have in order to impress the examiner.

- **Accurate and relevant legal content.** The ability to identify the law that is relevant to the problem question and provide a concise and accurate statement of that law to provide a foundation for your answer is one of the skills that is being tested in a problem question. Remember that a problem question requires only a statement of the current law and not an exploration of what the law was in the past or what it may be in the future.

- **A methodical approach to problem solving.** Far too many answers to problem questions start with a discussion of an obvious issue that stands out on the facts rather than starting with the first issue and working systematically through the requirements of the relevant law. A methodical approach also reduces the risk that you will overlook important issues and it should help you to produce a structured answer to the question.

- **Balanced arguments.** Try not to present a one-sided argument that only considers one possible outcome. Look for a counter-argument on every point that you make to create a balanced answer and then evaluate which of the competing arguments is more persuasive. Of course, it will not always be possible to find a counter-argument on every issue, but you should always look to see if one does exist.

- **Effective use of the facts.** The application of the law to the facts is the key skill at the heart of a successful answer to a problem question. Look for evidence in the facts to support every argument that you make. Try to incorporate sufficient facts into your answer so that it can be understood by someone who has not read the question.

- **Reference to case law to support arguments.** Case law can be used to explain the law, but it can also be used to really good effect to demonstrate how the law is likely to apply to the facts of the problem.

As these points illustrate, knowledge of the relevant law is only one aspect of a successful answer to a problem question. Problem solving is an inherently skills-based activity that is designed to test your ability to take the law and predict how it will apply to the facts before you.

 Lecturer viewpoint

Problem questions are far more popular in exams than essays, probably because the facts give the students so many clues about the right area of law. What students don't seem to understand is that the success or otherwise of their answer rests on whether they have mastered the problem-solving technique. I tell my students that a good answer to a problem question is 50 per cent legal knowledge and 50 per cent legal skills.

Although views may differ amongst lecturers regarding the relative contribution of knowledge and skills, there is general agreement that the two must combine to create an effective answer to a problem question. The good news is that the skills that are central to successful problem solving can be acquired and polished well before you reach the exam room. You should have had an opportunity to practise problem solving in coursework and by preparing answers for tutorial discussion. This chapter will build upon this by providing a step-by-step explanation of how these skills can be put into play within the time constraints of an exam, thus preparing you to produce a methodical answer that will attract good marks from the examiner.

◼ The nature of problem questions

Problem questions were developed as a means of assessment in law in order to simulate the process of a solicitor giving advice to a client. Take a minute to think about what a solicitor does when a client comes to him for advice:

- He gathers all the facts and sifts through them to decide which are relevant and which are irrelevant.

- He identifies the legal issues that are raised by the facts so that he can look up the relevant provisions of statute and case law.

■ He decides how the law applies to the facts so that he can give advice to the client.

A good answer to a problem question should demonstrate these skills. In the sections that follow, you will find guidance on how to analyse the facts, formulate the issues and use the law and the facts in combination in order to determine the likely outcome of the case.

■ Analysing the facts

The first step in producing a successful answer to a problem question involves working through the facts to ensure that you have a clear idea of what has happened. You should read the facts through at least twice, making a note of facts that seem to be significant, to ensure that you have not missed anything important. As you do so, make a list of events that seem important and try to establish the order in which events occurred, as this is often relevant.

Who is the focus of the question?

Start by identifying the person (or people) whose interests you are asked to assess. You will find this information in the instructions at the bottom of the set of facts. In most problem questions, you will either be looking at events from the perspective of someone who may have incurred legal liability, in which case you are concerned with what they have done and the claims that can be made against them as a result, or from the point of view of someone who has suffered harm or loss and wishes to make a claim, in which case you are interested in what has happened to them and who is responsible.

> **EXAM TIP**
>
> Lecturers often use the instructions at the end of the facts to limit the scope of the answer. For example, you might have a set of facts in which three people suffer injury as a result of a person's negligence, but you will only be instructed to explore the claims of two of them. Likewise, a problem question in criminal law may involve the commission of a range of different offences, but carry an instruction only to discuss liability for homicide offences. It is essential that you adhere to such instructions as there are no marks at all available for discussion of matters that are expressly excluded by the instructions.

Material facts, context and red herrings

A problem question is made up of a selection of pieces of information about the parties and events that have occurred. Your first task is to sift through the information provided and extract the material facts: that is, the facts that are relevant to the legal claims. A problem question tests your ability to differentiate between material facts and facts that merely provide the setting in which a claim has arisen.

The best method for doing this is to read every sentence carefully and question why each piece of information that it contains has been provided. Make a list of the facts and ask yourself 'Does it make a difference?' in relation to each of them. If you are unsure, assess whether legal liability would be different if a particular fact was changed or if it were removed from the problem altogether, as this will help you to decide whether it does make a difference. For example, if you are told that the events occurred on a particularly hot and sunny day, think about whether your view of the facts would be different if you did not know about the weather or if it was raining/snowing/cloudy. It may be that information about the weather is provided to 'set the scene' and has no relevance, but it may be significant to events that occur. For instance, if you discover that someone smashed a car window to release a dog then the weather is relevant as it may give rise to a defence.

The following facts should always be considered carefully as they are often material:

- The age of any of the parties.
- The time of day that events occurred.
- The location of the action.
- The occupation of the parties.
- The relationship of the parties to each other.

It is usually the case that you will not be told why a particular piece of information is significant. You will need to work this out for yourself by considering the requirements of the law and making reasonable deductions about the facts in question. For example, if a person's age is specified, you should think about whether the law applies differently in relation to a person of that age, such as the greater duty imposed on landowners to protect against harm arising from things on their land that are particularly alluring to children in the tort of occupiers' liability. You should also think about the characteristics associated with people of the age specified that might be relevant to the problem question: for instance, young children may be less able to recognise the risks associated with their actions, whereas elderly people might have an increased vulnerability to particular types of injury.

Finally, you should look out for red herrings. These are pieces of information that have no bearing on the facts but which has been introduced in order to distract or mislead you. You might think that this is unfair, but red herrings are a different way of testing your knowledge. In essence, your knowledge of the law should enable you to identify that a piece of information is not relevant and you should either ignore it or, better still, dismiss it with a brief explanation that explains why it has no bearing on liability.

■ Formulating the issues

Once the facts have been analysed, it should be possible to identify the issues that need to be addressed in your answer. An issue is a question raised by the facts that needs to be answered by reference to the relevant law. It is comprised of a statement that a particular event has occurred followed by the identification of the potential ground of legal liability that this raises. In essence, the issue matches a factual event with a relevant area of law as the following examples illustrate:

- Peter stabbed John during a heated argument during a golf tournament. John died three days later in hospital so Peter may be liable for murder.

- Penny has claimed that she needs to drive across Dawn's land in order to access the public highway from her house. As Dawn is not prepared to permit this, Penny will need to establish that an easement exists in her favour to secure access to the road.

- Lorraine has been refused a permit to park outside her house by the local authority who claim that she does not satisfy their 'exceptional need' requirements. She wishes to challenge this decision by way of judicial review.

Most problem questions will contain several different issues, each of which needs to be identified and addressed, but there will be occasions when a problem question will raise a single, particularly complicated, issue. Each issue should form a significant part of your answer and should be addressed in its totality before you move on to another issue.

Identifying sub-issues

Each issue raises a 'big' question that needs to be answered that corresponds to whether a party has liability or the basis of a successful claim. This issue needs to be broken down into a series of smaller sub-issues based upon the requirements of the law. In other words, in order to establish that a party has a claim or liability in relation to a particular area of law, there are a number of things that need to be established. Each head of liability in law should be broken down into its component parts and each should be established separately.

Figure 9.1 Issues and sub-issues

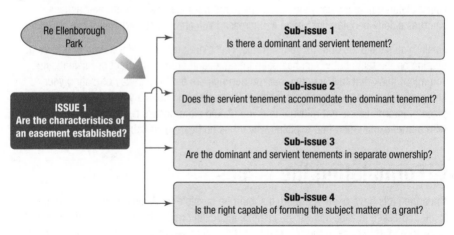

For example, your first issue might be whether the exercise of a right over another person's property can amount to an easement, in which case you would divide this into four sub-issues based upon the criteria set out in case law, as illustrated in Figure 9.1.

Dealing with the law

The law provides the foundation of your answer to a problem question. The standard advice that is given on how to answer a problem question is that you should state the law and then apply it to the facts. This is sound advice, as this approach allows you to demonstrate your knowledge to establish the requirements of the law followed by your skill in applying the law to determine whether the requirements of the law are satisfied. It is important to remember that this involves two distinct skills that should be demonstrated separately, as Figure 9.2 illustrates.

Figure 9.2 Stating and applying the law

State the law		Apply the law to the facts
Appropriation is defined by section 3 of the Theft Act 1968 as the assumption of the rights of the owner. In *R* v. *Gomez*, it was held that this involved an assumption of any one of the rights of the owner, rather than all of the rights, and that this could occur even if the owner had given his consent to the appropriation.		Annabelle has taken the reference book from the library and hidden it in her bag in order to remove it. This is an appropriation as only the owner of the book has the right to remove it from the shelf and alter its location. It is immaterial that the library gives implied consent to users to remove books from the shelf as an appropriation can occur with consent and, in any case, the library would not have consented to the removal of a reference-only copy from the library.

There are three ways in which the law is used when answering problem questions, each of which will be discussed in the sections that follow:

■ As a source of a legal principle.

■ To elaborate on the meaning of a word or phrase.

■ To demonstrate the operation of the law.

Source of legal principle

Every piece of law that you encounter during your studies has its source in some document such as a statute, a statutory instrument, a principle of international law, a regulation or directive from Europe or the case law of the courts. The place where this law was first written down or otherwise enunciated is its source. It is expected that you will identify the source of all the law that you use in your answers to problem questions. This requires that you provide an abstract statement of the law that also identifies the source of that legal rule such as:

■ Theft is defined by section 1 of the Theft Act 1968 as the dishonest appropriation of property belonging to another with the intention to permanently deprive.

■ In *Council of Civil Service Unions* v. *Minister for the Civil Service* (the *GCHQ* case), the House of Lords identified three grounds of judicial review: illegality, irrationality and procedural impropriety.

■ The right to a fair trial is set out in Article 6 of the European Convention on Human Rights and this includes the right of a person accused of a criminal offence to be presumed innocent until proven guilty (Article 6(2)).

> **EXAM TIP**
>
> Do not waste time writing out long extracts from the statute. If you have a statute book in the exam, all you are demonstrating to the examiner is that you can copy from a book and that is not very impressive! If your institution does not permit statute books in the exam room, you would not want to clog up your memory with the words of a statute when there are far more useful things that you could commit to memory. Instead, make sure you can paraphrase the relevant statutory provision in a way that captures its essential meaning.

Elaboration on meaning

It is often necessary to move beyond a bald statement of what the law is into a more detailed exploration of its meaning. This may involve using additional sources to supplement that used when stating the legal principle; for example, you might state the legal principle as set out in statute and then use case law to elaborate on its meaning. You can see this demonstrated in Figure 9.2 where the basic definition found in section 3 is supplemented by reference to case law that has interpreted this statutory provision.

Remember, though, that you should only elaborate on the meaning of words and phrases if it is necessary to do so. In other words, stick to simple statements of law unless the facts are such that the issue cannot be resolved without a more detailed exploration of the meaning of the law.

Example: Unnecessary elaboration

In the extracts that follow, you will see a typical example of unnecessary elaboration that is followed by a reformulation of the same point, but in a more suitable level of detail. The final example shows a situation when elaboration on the basic meaning would be appropriate.

Unnecessary elaboration

Section 4 of the Theft Act 1968 defines property to include 'money and all other property, real or personal, including things in action and other intangible property'. Section 4 also states that the following do not fall within the meaning of property: land, plants that are growing in the wild (unless picked for commercial purposes) and wild creatures. What is more, it was held in *Oxford* v. *Moss* that confidential information is not property for the purposes of theft. Deborah has taken Alison's laptop from her room and this would fall within section 4 as personal property so this element of theft is satisfied.

Concise and focused alternative

As the issue is a straightforward one, it could have been dealt with in a single sentence:

The definition of 'property' in section 4 of the Theft Act 1968 covers all property 'real and personal' so would include the laptop taken by Deborah.

Necessary elaboration

Section 4 of the Theft Act 1968 defines property to include 'money and all other property, real and personal'. However, section 4(3) goes on to say that mushrooms, flowers, fruit and foliage growing wild will not fall within the definition of property unless it was done for reward or resale. Pippa has picked apples from a tree that is growing wild in the woods. There is nothing to suggest that she intends to sell these apples, so it seems that they would not be regarded as property and she cannot be guilty of theft.

The sort of unnecessary elaboration seen in the first example is often the result of a determination to get all the law that has been learned down on paper in the exam. Students often explain that they feel like all the effort of learning the law is wasted if it is not included in the exam. This is understandable, but you do need to remember that irrelevant content will not attract any marks and may actually reduce the quality of your answer and result in lower marks. This is because it gives the examiner the impression that the content of your answers is determined by memory rather than knowledge. Examiners will be far more impressed if you are able to select only relevant points from the wealth of law that you have learned for inclusion in your answer.

Another similar problem involves the inclusion of detail about the historical evolution of the law and proposals for future reform.

 Lecturer viewpoint

Some students treat problem questions as if they were essays and produce several pages of the history and background of a piece of law when it could be captured in one or two sentences. I just think 'oh dear, what a waste of time' as I draw a line through that part of the answer and write 'essay in disguise' in the margin.

Avoid the temptation to produce an 'essay in disguise' by ensuring that you only provide a statement of the current law as it is relevant to the facts in your answers. In other words, do not concern yourself with what the law once was or what it might be in the future, as these points belong in an essay, not in an answer to a problem question. As noted earlier in this chapter, a problem question is a simulation of a solicitor–client consultation; if you visit a solicitor, you want to know how the law as it is today applies to your situation. You would not be impressed with a solicitor who outlined every legal development in the past 20 years or speculated about what would happen to your case if the law changed in the future. Try to remember this when explaining the law in a problem question and aim to produce concise statements of the current law.

EXAM TIP

Make sure that you mention the name of one of the parties in every paragraph. This will stop you from drifting off focus into an abstract description of the law.

Operation of the law

The final way in which the law can be used when answering problem questions is particular to case law and it involves using the facts of cases to demonstrate how the law might apply to the facts of the problem.

Once you have stated the law and engaged in any necessary elaboration of its meaning, you will need to apply the law to the facts. When doing this, you can use existing case law to substantiate your argument that a particular outcome is likely by showing how the law has been applied in a case with similar facts.

Example: Using case law to illustrate the operation of the law

Trish was hit by a car when she ran across a busy dual carriageway to escape from her boyfriend, Chris, who she thought was going to hit her during a heated argument. In *Roberts*, it was held that a defendant may be liable for causing injuries to a person that were sustained whilst escaping from a threat posed by the defendant provided that the victim's response was not 'so daft' as to be unforeseeable. It may be argued that Trish's actions in running across the road crossed that threshold and Chris will not be liable for her injuries. However, in *Lewis*, a husband was liable for injuries sustained by his wife when she jumped out of a first floor window to escape from him during an argument. This is not dissimilar to Trish's response in running across a busy road. Moreover, in *Roberts* itself, the defendant was liable for the victim's injuries that were sustained when she jumped from a moving car to avoid his sexual advances. In light of these cases, it seems reasonable to conclude that Chris will be held to have caused Trish's injuries as she was escaping from his threats when she was hit by a car.

Notice here that the answer emphasises the similarities between the facts of the case and the facts of the problem. This is important if you want to reach the same conclusion as was reached in the case. If, however, you wanted to conclude that Chris was not liable for Trish's injuries, you would need to distinguish the facts of the problem and the facts of the case: in other words, you would draw attention to their differences. For example, you could argue that running across a busy road is different from jumping from a window or out of a moving car because it carries a risk of far more serious injury, or even death, due to the high speeds at which the cars will be moving on a dual carriageway. This factor could put Trish's reaction into the category of responses that are 'so daft' that they are unforeseeable thus the defendant is not regarded as the cause of the injuries that result.

It is all down to how you use the facts from case law. Emphasise similarities if you want to reach the same conclusion as the case and highlight distinguishing factors if you want to reach a difference conclusion.

■ Applying the law

This is the most important aspect of problem solving. Without application of the law to the facts, all you have done is to identify and explain the relevant law. This is not that difficult and all it does is demonstrate that you are able to memorise, recall and write out legal principles. It is the application of the law to the facts that demonstrates that you understand how the law works. The application stage of problem solving involves extracting evidence from the facts provided that the requirements of the law that you have explained have been satisfied or explaining why they are not satisfied. If you do not do this, you are failing to demonstrate the key skill involved in problem solving and your answer will be weak as a result.

Lecturer viewpoint

I get really frustrated by students who do not apply the law properly. After all, the facts are provided for them in the problem and all they have to do is pick them out and write them down. I get particularly annoyed by sweeping statements such as 'it is obvious that this is established' without any mention of the facts that lead to this conclusion.

It is essential that you incorporate sufficient facts into your answer to enable you to demonstrate your ability to apply the law to the facts.

- Get into the habit of looking for evidence in the facts to support every point that you make in your answer.

- Circle or highlight facts in the question that you want to include in your answer.

- Be systematic when planning your answer. If the law has three requirements then look for three facts that match them.

- Be specific in your use of the facts. Identify particular facts from the question and write them in your answer.

- Avoid general statements that it is clear/obvious/apparent that the requirements of the law are satisfied. This is a conclusion, not a demonstration of the application of the law to the facts.

STUDENT EXPERIENCE

The first thing I do is read through a problem question and make a quick list of all the facts that I think are significant, then I number them in the order that I think I'll use them in my answer and tick them off as I write. When my answer is finished, I read through and make another list of all the facts that I've included. I compare this with my first list to make sure that I've put all the facts in that needed to be included and, if not, I try to add them into my answer.

David

Create balanced arguments

It is important to remember to look at both sides of the argument in relation to each sub-issue wherever possible. Bear in mind that your task is to assess the strength of the claims or liability that potentially arise on the facts of a problem question. Even if the instruction that accompanies the facts is to advise a particular party, that does not mean that you should only include points that support their argument; you will need to consider the case against them too in order to ensure that you reach a balanced conclusion as to their potential liability or the strength of their claim.

You might find that it helps you to create a balanced argument if you set out the points for and against each issue that you address when you are planning your answer. In the table below, you will see this done in relation to a problem question dealing with gross negligence liability. As you can see, this approach enables you to see at a glance whether you need to make a counter-argument in your answer. It also helps you to understand the flow of your argument before you start to write your full answer. The notes set out in the table also make use of specific facts from the problem: you have not seen the question, but it should be possible to get a clear idea of what has happened from the points noted for inclusion in the answer. This is the level of detail to aim for in your answers.

Elements of liability	Arguments for	Arguments against	Conclusion
Does Oliver have a duty of care? This is established using ordinary principles of negligence.	He is a qualified electrician who has been engaged to install Rachel's hot tub. A contractual duty of care exists.	None	Duty of care established.
Has Oliver breached that duty? Has he fallen below the standards expected of the reasonable competent professional?	The hot tub was wired incorrectly. Oliver realised that he had bought the incorrect wiring diagram to the job but thought that he could remember it. A reasonably competent electrician, knowing the dangers of electricity and water, would have gone back home to collect the wiring diagram rather than hoping that he could remember it.	Oliver has been an electrician for 20 years and has installed a large number of hot tubs. He was convinced that he could remember the correct wiring sequence. It is possible that all other electricians would have relied on their memory and knowledge in the circumstances rather than going home to collect the wiring diagram.	Arguable either way, but it is likely that he will be held to have breached his duty of care.

▶

Did the breach of duty cause death? Ordinary principles of factual and legal causation apply.	'But for' the faulty wiring, Rachel would not have been electrocuted in the hot tub on the first occasion that she used it. There are no competing causes of death.	None.	Causation established.
Does this go beyond civil liability and merit the imposition of criminal liability?	Oliver rushed the job, did it incorrectly and death occurred as a result. He considered going home to get the wiring diagram so he was aware that he might need it but he did not want to fall behind with his work schedule.	Oliver was in a hurry because he wanted to visit his son who was seriously ill in hospital, so the jury may feel sympathy for him. He has never made any serious errors in his 20 years as an electrician.	Although the jury might be sympathetic because of his son's illness, it is unlikely that they will decide that this justifies acquitting him of manslaughter.

EXAM TIP

If you write practice answers to problem questions as a part of your revision, use this as an opportunity to test whether you are including sufficient facts in your answer. Ask a friend to summarise the events that occurred in the question just from reading your answer. In other words, see if they can work backwards from your answer to predict the question. If their summary of the problem has significant gaps, you will know that you are not doing enough to apply the law to the specific facts of the problem.

■ Common problems

In this final section of the chapter, the focus will be on the weaknesses that often arise in problem questions written in exams, along with some suggestions as to how to avoid such weaknesses in your own work. Three of the most common problems have already been covered in the earlier sections of this chapter so these are just listed here as a reminder. Look back at the relevant section for details of how to avoid making these mistakes in the exam:

- Too much description and the inclusion of irrelevant detail.
- Answers that do not include any or enough authority.
- Weak or vague application of the law to the facts.

Repeating the facts

Although it is essential to the success of an answer to a problem question that the facts are included in the answer, this does not mean that they should be copied out or paraphrased at the start of the answer. It is often the case that the first paragraph or, in extreme cases, the first page of an answer is devoted to a summary of the facts. This is not a good approach as it does not demonstrate any skill to the examiner and it is certainly not an acceptable means of ensuring that sufficient facts are contained in your answer. Make sure that your answer does not contain large chunks of the facts any more than it does large chunks of the law. The trick to success is to incorporate the law and the facts together in short bursts.

Muddled answers

A lack of structure is a serious problem for many answers. This often arises as a result of a lack of planning. Students who start writing their answers immediately without analysing the question and planning their answer tend to jump straight in to tackle an issue that is really obvious; for example, it might be something that stands out because it is similar to the facts of a case or is reminiscent of an issue discussed in a tutorial. It is important to take time to identify all the issues that need to be covered and to plan out a structure for the answer. This reduces the risk that issues will be missed out and creates a methodical answer that develops in a logical manner which makes it easy for the examiner to follow your reasoning.

Omission of important issues

Lack of planning can also lead to answers that do not identify all of the issues. Of course, it is sometimes the case that you will simply not recognise all of the issues but reduce the risk of this happening by ensuring that you read the problem sentence-by-sentence and write down the points that occur to you, rather than skimming through it to see what it is about in general terms.

Lack of logical reasoning

Students sometimes start with a clear idea of what outcome they should reach on a particular issue based upon an instinctive evaluation of the facts. They then try to shape their answer in order to reach that conclusion, which is a problem if the facts do not actually support the conclusion that they want to reach.

> **Lecturer viewpoint**
>
> Students think that problem questions are about getting the right answer. They don't realise that it is a test of their reasoning. They see something in a problem question that reminds them of a case and assume that it must have the same outcome. They don't realise that we deliberately create problem questions so that they are similar to decided cases but with a twist in the facts that means that the outcome is different to the case. If they would only start with the building blocks of liability and work their way through logically then they wouldn't fall into the trap.

This demonstrates the perils of pre-judging the outcome of a problem question. Try not to start with an assumption of the conclusion but instead work through the elements of the relevant law in a methodical manner and accept the conclusion that this produces. You should find that creating a plan of your answer helps you to create a logical line of argument based upon the facts rather than on your preconceptions of the correct outcome.

Abdication of responsibility

A good answer to a problem question should conclude with a reasoned summary of your findings with regards to the party's liability or the strength of their claim. However, students often avoid reaching a conclusion about liability and instead pepper their answers with phrases such as 'this will be for the court to decide' or 'this is a question for the jury'. That may well be the case in practice, but in the context of a problem question it is for you to weigh up the arguments that you have presented and make a prediction as to the likely outcome of the case. When you abdicate responsibility for reaching a conclusion to a fictional court or jury, you are depriving yourself of the opportunity to demonstrate to the examiner that you are able to determine which of the competing arguments that you have presented is most likely to succeed.

Failure to reach a conclusion

Many answers to problem questions just stop abruptly with no attempt to summarise the liability or claims that have been established. The reason for this is often that students are not sure that they have reached the right conclusion or because they have not been able to reach a decision one way or the other.

Your answer should always have a conclusion. If, as is often the case, the facts are not sufficiently clear-cut to allow you to reach a definite conclusion, it is perfectly acceptable to reach a contingent or 'if' conclusion. This is a statement that a particular conclusion is possible *if* a certain condition exists or a specific fact can be proven. You may also draw attention to any obstacles that will prevent this outcome from being reached. These are examples of a contingent conclusion:

- Georgia will be able to use money from the trust created by her father if she can convince the trustees that this expenditure is necessary for her to continue her education. However, as the university provides accommodation for all its students, her arguments may not persuade the trustees that money should be spent this way.

- Llewellyn will be liable for rape unless he can convince the jury that it was reasonable for him to believe that Mary was consenting to intercourse even though she was so intoxicated that she could not stand up.

- There seems to be little basis upon which Margaret can avoid being liable for negligence after setting fire to Ivor's house. Her argument that the spread of the fire was not foreseeable seems unconvincing in light of the proximity of the buildings.

Analysing a problem answer

 Try this

Spotting errors and weaknesses

This chapter has provided guidelines on producing a focused and methodical answer to a problem question. It has also highlighted common faults that occur in answers to problem questions and made suggestions as to how these can be avoided. Test your ability to create an effective answer to a problem question by spotting the errors and weaknesses with the answer provided below and correcting them to create a stronger answer. You will find an improved version of the answer on the Companion Website along with an explanation of the way in which it was strengthened.

Problem question on statutory interpretation

Following concerns about suffering caused to animals by negligent owners, the government introduced new animal welfare legislation with tougher penalties. Section 1 of the Domestic Animals Protection Act 2010 (fictitious) states that the owner of an animal will be guilty of a criminal offence if the animal is caused avoidable suffering or is not kept in conditions that are conducive to its good health and well-being. Section 10 provides that 'animal' includes dogs, cats, rabbits, hamsters, rats, mice, horses, donkeys and other pets. Section 12 of the Act states that the owner of an animal is any person aged 16 or over who has purchased, been given or otherwise acquired an animal.

Connor is a retired vet who lives in an isolated cottage in the middle of the countryside. He discovers a fox that has been hit by a car and takes it home to treat its injuries. He makes a nest for it in his shed and it takes up residence there once its injuries are healed. Connor takes it food every night. A homeless man breaks into the shed one night, looking for somewhere to sleep, and is bitten by the fox. He tells the nurse treating him at the hospital how his injury was caused and she alerts the authorities. A policeman visits Connor to remove the fox and notify him that he is likely to be prosecuted under section 1 of the Act keeping the fox in unsuitable conditions.

Considering different approaches to statutory interpretation, determine whether Connor will incur liability under the Domestic Animals Protection Act.

Answer

There are a number of different approaches to statutory interpretation including the literal rule and the mischief rule. The literal rule gives words used their ordinary everyday meaning and the mischief rule looks at the problem that the law was introduced to remedy. There are also rules of language such as the *ejusdem generis* rule that deals with the interpretation of lists.

Connor may be liable under section 1 of the Domestic Animals Protection Act 2010 because he has caused the fox unnecessary suffering. A fox is a wild animal so it should not be kept in a shed. Even though Connor has not shut it in the shed, he is keeping it there by providing a ready source of food and shelter. The fox attacked the tramp because he was cornered in territory that he had come to consider as his own, which is also within the meaning of unnecessary suffering.

The first question to consider is whether a fox falls within the definition of 'animal' found in section 10 of the Act. This section provides a list of creatures that do fall within the Act and it does not include a fox. However, the literal interpretation of 'animal' would probably include a fox. The mischief rule looks at the problem that the law was introduced to address. Here, it was the problem of negligent owners causing suffering to their pets. If the purpose of the law was to penalise people who cause suffering to animals then it is likely that it will cover Connor.

The next issue to consider is whether the *ejusdem generis* rule would include a fox within the statutory definition of an animal. This approach provides that where a general term is added at the end of a list of specific examples, the general term should be interpreted only to include other things that are similar in nature to the specific examples provided. In *Powell* v. *Kempton Park Racecourse*, it was held that legislation that prohibited gambling in a house, office, room or other place did not cover an outdoor gambling ring because the other places listed shared a common characteristic of being indoors. The legislation provides a list of common domestic pets such as dogs, cats and horses. By contrast, a fox is a wild animal that is very rarely tamed and kept as a pet. If this approach is taken, a fox would not fall within the ambit of the legislation and Connor cannot be liable.

The final point to consider is whether Connor has kept the fox in unsuitable conditions. Connor is a retired vet. This means that he has spent his life caring for and healing animals, so he is probably far better placed to decide what living conditions are suitable for an injured fox than a policeman who has no such expertise with animals. It is also established that Connor is aged 16 or above as he would not be a qualified vet otherwise.

There are arguments for and against Connor's liability, but it seems as if it would be unfair to hold him liable as the fox is visiting the shed of its own accord.

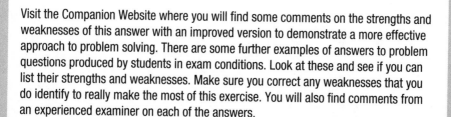

www.pearsoned.co.uk/lawexpress

■ To find out more ...

Visit the Companion Website where you will find some comments on the strengths and weaknesses of this answer with an improved version to demonstrate a more effective approach to problem solving. There are some further examples of answers to problem questions produced by students in exam conditions. Look at these and see if you can list their strengths and weaknesses. Make sure you correct any weaknesses that you do identify to really make the most of this exercise. You will also find comments from an experienced examiner on each of the answers.

NOTES

NOTES

Exploiting feedback

Revision checklist

Topics covered in this chapter:

- [ ] Method of feedback available on exam performance
- [ ] Using other forms of feedback to strengthen exam performance
- [ ] Understanding comments
- [ ] Responding to and learning from feedback

Introduction

Feedback is a reaction to your work by the person responsible for marking it. Positive feedback will identify the things that you have done well, whilst negative feedback focuses on the problems with your work such as omissions, inaccuracy or lack of a particular skill. Both kinds of feedback are valuable in enabling you to improve your work in the future. It is often difficult to receive feedback on your answers to exam questions, so the aim of this chapter is to suggest ways in which you can make the most of feedback from other sources to help you strengthen your exam performance.

Feedback on exam performance

It is still quite unusual for students to be given individual feedback on their performance in exams other than the overall mark awarded for each paper. This is unfortunate from the point of view of the student as knowledge of the mark informs you whether your overall performance was as good as you had hoped, but it gives you no insight into which answers were most successful and it does not help you to understand what you did well and where further work is needed. Without this information, it is difficult to formulate a strategy to improve your performance in subsequent exams.

Some universities have adopted policies to provide a greater level of feedback on exam performance:

- **Publication of generic feedback.** This is a summary of the performance of all students taking a particular exam which notes, for instance, the range of marks awarded for the paper as a whole and for individual questions, the frequency with which each question was answered and any common problems that emerged. This offers only limited insight into individual performance. For example, you might find out that one of the questions that you answered was not done well by many students and generally received lower marks. This will help you to understand your mark, but it does give you a great deal of information on your own performance that will help you to do better in future.

- **Provision of insight into the answers.** This might take the form of a complete model answer, a list of bullet points that should have appeared in each answer or a set of annotated answers that explains how the question should have been tackled. This sort of feedback can be useful as it provides a basis for comparison with your own answers. This is particularly useful if you are given copies of your own exam answers but this is not a widespread practice so you may have to rely on your memory.

- **One-to-one discussion of exam performance.** It may be possible to obtain a copy of your exam paper and discuss this with the marker or another lecturer such as your personal tutor. This enables you to gain direct insight into what you did well and what was less successful in your answers, thus providing you with a basis to make changes in order to improve in future exams.

- **Opportunity to see your answers.** You may be able to see or even obtain a copy of the answers that you produced in the exam. This gives you an opportunity to revisit your work and evaluate it away from the pressure of the exam so you may be able to see defects in your own work. If you are permitted to take a copy of your answers, you can spend time analysing them and working out what you should have done differently. There may be comments from the examiner that will help you to identify the strengths and weaknesses of your answers.

 Lecturer viewpoint

Any comments that I write on an exam script are intended to explain my mark to the second marker or external examiner so they are blunt compared to the comments that I would write on coursework. Students asking to see their marked exam papers should be aware of this so that they are prepared to see comments such as 'waffle', 'regurgitated without thought' or 'nonsense' written on their answers.

If any of these sources of feedback are available at your university then make sure that you take full advantage of them. One of the key reasons that students perform less well than they would like in the exams can be explained by lack of feedback. If you do not know what it is that you did in your first year exams that led to disappointing marks, you will not appreciate that you need to make a change in order to achieve greater success. Knowing what you did wrong is half the battle in putting it right so do take every opportunity to obtain feedback on your performance.

EXAM TIP

If your university has a policy which states that students will have an opportunity to obtain feedback on exam performance or to see their marked papers, this might mean that it is available, but only if you ask to do so. Find out what the rules are at your university to ensure that you know what feedback is available and what you need to do to obtain it.

Other sources of feedback

If your university does not provide feedback on your exams, you will need to focus on the other forms of feedback that are available and consider how these can be used to improve your exam performance. In the sections that follow, you will find details of different types of feedback that you may receive during the course of your studies along with suggestions as to how this can be useful to you in terms of strengthening the answers that you produce in the exams.

Coursework marks

The mark that your work receives is a simple form of feedback and it is the one that gives the most immediate indication of the success or otherwise of your work.

Universities vary in the way that they grade coursework and exams with some using percentages and others using bands such as A, B, C, D or Pass, Merit and Distinction to indicate the quality of your work. Obviously, a numeric approach is most useful as a measure of your performance: for example, if you receive a mark of 60 per cent, you know that you only just made it into the upper second class band whereas 69 per cent tells you that your work was almost of first class standard. By contrast, both pieces of work would fall into the same band.

Irrespective of the approach taken to grading work at your university, you will be able to compare your performance in coursework and in the exams. You should aim to achieve marks within the same band in both forms of assessment. Many students consider that exams are harder than coursework – probably due to the time constraints and the need to remember the law – but exam questions are tailored to work in exam conditions and are marked according to a different set of criteria to coursework, so there should not really be any great discrepancy in marks.

 Lecturer viewpoint

Exams are not harder than coursework: they just test different skills. If students get lower marks in the exams, this is because they are not demonstrating the knowledge and skills that the exam is designed to test.

In essence, if your exam marks are lower than your coursework marks then this is a sign that there is some weakness in the way that you revise or the way that you answer questions in the exam. Hopefully, as you are reading this book, you will be able to make some changes and improve your performance in the exams so that you are able to achieve marks that are on par with your coursework performance.

Feedback sheets

Most universities provide feedback on coursework by way of a printed sheet that sets out a series of competences and indicates the extent to which students have achieved these by ticking a box as illustrated in Figure 10.1.

Figure 10.1 Sample assessment criteria

	Poor	Below average	Satisfactory	Good	Excellent
Knowledge of the relevant law	☐	☐	☐	☐	☐
Application to the question	☐	☐	☐	☐	☐
Use of supporting authority	☐	☐	☐	☐	☐
Written style, grammar and punctuation	☐	☐	☐	☐	☐

Take time to look how well you performed according to the tick boxes. Any area that was not marked as excellent or good indicates that there is an area in need of improvement. Of course, some of these boxes will be specific to the particular piece of assessment: if you did not score well on 'understanding the law' then perhaps this was just a tricky area for you rather than a cause of general concern. However, if you were to see this replicated on a number of forms for different pieces of work then there is clearly a more general problem that needs to be addressed.

✓ **Try this**

Identify areas that need work

1 Collect together all the feedback sheets for the academic year and list all the categories: for example, excellent, good, satisfactory, unsatisfactory, very poor.

2 Create a frequency chart that records how often you score in each of these categories. How does your overall profile look? Is your work mostly excellent/good or are you receiving the majority of ticks in the satisfactory box? This gives you an idea of how well you are performing across your assessments and it might look something like this:

Excellent	IIIII I					6
Good	IIIII IIIII IIIII					15
Satisfactory	IIIII IIIII IIIII IIIII IIIII					25
Unsatisfactory	IIIII II					7
Poor	IIII					4

3   Now list each of the marking criteria. Work through each feedback sheet and give yourself a mark of 5 every time you receive a distinction, 4 for a good and so on down to 1 mark for unsatisfactory. Add these up to see your total for each of the criteria.

Accuracy of legal content $5 + 3 + 3 + 3 + 1 = 15$

Quality of argument $3 + 2 + 3 + 2 + 1 = 11$

Structure of argument $1 + 1 + 2 + 1 + 2 = 7$

4   Now relist the marking criteria starting with your lowest overall total as this will enable you to identify the areas where most work is needed, thereby enabling you to prioritise the areas of greatest weakness. This might look something like this:

Clarity of written expression   6

Structure of argument   7

Evidence of research   8

5   Consider whether and, if so, how each of these is likely to effect exam performance. Using the advice provided in this book and other sources as appropriate, decide on ways to improve on areas of weakness.

Written comments

Some lecturers will provide written comments on your coursework that can be used to gain insight into your strengths and weaknesses that might affect your exam performance. The value of such written comments is that they are a specific response to something in your work rather than a general comment on your performance as they are written alongside the point to which they relate. This will enable you to pinpoint the strengths and weaknesses of your own work far more accurately than is possible from tick boxes or comments written on a feedback sheet.

Verbal feedback

Try to get into the habit of talking to your lecturers. You could ask for their views on your general understanding of a topic based upon your contribution to tutorial discussion or ask them for further feedback on a particular piece of work that they have marked. Make sure that you approach this in a constructive manner by emphasising that you want to gain a clearer understanding of where your work could be improved: lecturers are most reluctant to engage with students who want to discuss their work with a view to arguing that it should have received a better mark. Try to make sure that you come away from such a meeting with information that makes a positive contribution to your desire to perform better in the exams: you could ask the lecturer to identify the three priority areas that need attention, for example, or to provide some concrete examples of how a particular area of weakness could be improved.

You could also obtain verbal feedback by asking a lecturer to comment on a practice answer that you have written (see Chapter 3). This can be of great value if you have produced your answer in exam conditions, i.e. a handwritten answer produced without notes and within time constraints. This will be particularly useful if your university does not permit access to answers that you have written in the exams.

■ Understanding feedback comments

Feedback on coursework is aimed at students. It is intended to provide you with an understanding of the strengths and weaknesses of your work. It should also be constructive, which means that it should explain what is wrong and offer suggestions on how it could be put right or how a problem could be avoided in the future. Therefore, in a perfect world, the feedback that you receive should allow you to understand why you received the mark that you did and how you would improve your work in order to obtain better marks in the future.

Marking shorthand

Unfortunately, the time pressures involved in marking a large volume of coursework means that markers do not always have the opportunity to provide comprehensive feedback. As a result, markers develop a form of shorthand for feedback that uses words, phrases and sometimes symbols to communicate their views about your work. This can lead to feedback that is not readily understood by students so the sections that follow will demystify some of the more common comments that you might find on your work and explain how the weaknesses that they indicate can be improved.

Structure

The word 'structure' (written with or without an exclamation mark) indicates that there is something wrong with the way in which your work is organised. In essence, the marker thinks that there is a problem with the order in which you have presented the points that make up your work. They may use arrows to indicate where they think that the point that you have made should appear in your work.

A good structure is the foundation of a successful exam answer. Adverse comments about structure in coursework should ring loud warning bells alerting you to the need to work on this important feature for the exam. If you cannot structure your coursework, given that you have time to plan it and can move paragraphs around with ease on your computer, then it is likely that you will really struggle in the exam where time is short and you need to get the structure right first time as you are producing handwritten answers.

Overcome these problems by creating plans of your answers in the exams as this tends to lead to a stronger structure than those produced by students who start writing without any idea of how their answer is going to develop. Chapters 8 and 9 emphasise the value of planning your answers in the exam and offer advice on constructing a quick and effective answer plan.

Vague

Words such as 'vague' or 'unclear' indicate that the way that your answer is expressed is too general and that you needed to be more precise and to express your ideas with greater clarity. In essence, your marker is saying 'I do not understand what you have written here so I suspect that you may not understand the law'. Imprecision and lack of clarity of expression are actually a failure of your written style but can give the impression that there is a failure of knowledge. Make sure that you avoid this problem in the exam by working to develop a mode of expression that allows you to communicate your understanding of the law in very clear terms.

> **EXAM TIP**
>
> Problems with clarity of expression often arise from the misuse of words. Students who are keen to use sophisticated language in their answers sometimes fall into difficulty if they do not have a correct grasp of how a particular word should be used. Remember, it is better to use simple language and be understood than it is to use more complex language at the expense of clarity.

Of course, it may be that your work was vague because you did not have a sufficient understanding of the law. Avoid this problem by filling in any gaps in your knowledge during the revision period.

So what?

This indicates that the marker does not understand the relevance of your point. This is also sometimes expressed by 'relevance?'. This could either mean that the point is not relevant and should not have been included in your answer or that it is relevant but your answer should have gone on to explain how it was relevant.

Avoid the inclusion of irrelevant material in the exam by taking a few minutes to create a plan of your answer. Not only will this help to strengthen your structure (see above) but it will give you the opportunity to test each point that you want to include for relevance. Remember that your points must be relevant to the specific question asked and not just to the topic of the question. There is more discussion of this issue in relation to the content of essays in Chapter 8.

Once you have decided that a point has sufficient relevance to be included in your answer, ensure that you make this clear to the marker by explaining its relevance. If you cannot tie your point in with the question, then it is not relevant and should not be included. Not only will relating each point to the question ensure that it is relevant and that its relevance is clear to the marker, it will also strengthen your answer as you will be using your content to answer the question.

And ...

A comment that consists of the word 'and' followed by an ellipsis (three dots) indicates that something is missing from your answer. If you encounter this in your coursework, look at your answer carefully to identify what it is that is missing, as this is a clue to the level of detail that your marker was expecting. This may help you to gauge the level of detail that is expected in the exam.

Exclamation marks

A marker will use an exclamation mark to indicate that there is something unusual, surprising or even shocking about a point that you have made in your answer. Try to work out what it is that has prompted this reaction and be sure to ask for clarification if you are unsure. An exclamation mark is very unlikely to be an indication that the marker approves of what you have written, so it is important that you find out what has led to its appearance in your work and avoid it in future.

Questions marks

A question mark that is not preceded by a question is a way of expressing lack of understanding. Your marker is telling you that he cannot work out what you mean or why you have made a particular point. This may be due to lack of clarity of expression or because the point that you have made is inaccurate or irrelevant.

Ticks

If you see a tick on your work, it can indicate that the marker is expressing approval of the point that you have made or that the point that you have made is accurate and relevant. However, it can just mean that the marker has read the page. Some markers do not like to write comments on your work so will simply put a tick on each page to show that it has been read. A tick that indicates approval will usually be alongside the relevant point whereas a tick to show that work has been read will generally be at the bottom of the page.

Crossing out

You may find that parts of your answer have been crossed out by the marker. This may be a word, a sentence a paragraph or, in extreme situations, several pages of your work. This indicates either that it is inaccurate or irrelevant. If there is no accompanying comment, you will need to ask the marker which of these was the problem as you will need to take different remedial steps to address inaccuracy than are needed to tackle irrelevance.

Gram., punct. and sp.

These are the abbreviations for grammar, punctuation and spelling and are used to indicate that there is an error in one of these particular areas. Students often overlook the importance of correct grammar, punctuation and spelling in the exams, thinking that correct content will be rewarded irrespective of how it is expressed. This is not the case. A high degree of technical inaccuracy in your work is likely to be penalised by the examiner and, in addition to this, will have a negative impact on the clarity of your writing, which may also lead to a reduction in marks. It is crucial that you aim for flawless expression in the exam so be alert for signs of problems in this area in your coursework and seek to strengthen your written style before the exam.

Reacting to comments

Hopefully, most of the comments on your coursework will be self-explanatory and, with the help of the guidelines above on deciphering marking shorthand, you will be able to understand all the positive and negative points that the marker has made about your work. The next consideration is how to respond to these comments.

 Lecturer viewpoint

There are three ways that students react to negative comments on their coursework. Some get angry and complain, either to the marker or about the marker. Some get upset and start to feel anxious about their studies and their prospects of success. And some students will understand that the comments were written to help rather than to criticise or undermine and come and ask for help to improve their work. These students are the ones who will produce better work next time.

It is never pleasant to receive negative feedback, especially if it is not limited to one or two points but instead picks up on problems throughout a piece of work and is accompanied by a low mark. It can be a good idea to leave it a day or two so that any feelings of disappointment and frustration have passed so that you can look at your work dispassionately and use the feedback to understand what went wrong and how to do better in future work.

If you have received a feedback form that uses tick boxes to indicate how well your essay has performed against particular criteria, carry out the exercise outlined earlier in this chapter to identify the aspects of your work that require particular attention. Supplement this with any comments that you have received, either on a comment box on the front sheet or on the work itself. These comments should help you to understand why at least some of the ticks were in boxes that indicated poor performance and may also give you some suggestions as to what you could have done differently. Take each problem area and think about how it will affect you in the exam and what you can do to prevent it happening (of course, you should also think about how you can avoid its reoccurrence in subsequent coursework, but the focus of this chapter is to help you to use feedback to improve your performance in the exams). You will find some suggestions to help you with this in the table below that sets out some of the commonest problems that occur in coursework and which can have a negative impact on the answers produced in the exam.

Problem in coursework	Impact on exam performance	Solution
Poor structure	Disorganised answers are common in exams. They limit the success of the answer as the examiner is looking for evidence of planning and a failure to present points in a logical order will interfere with your ability to present a flowing argument.	Plan your answer before you start writing. Make sure that you think about how each point will relate to the next so that your essay tells a story.
Lack of clarity	If the examiner cannot understand what you have written, he cannot give marks for it because he cannot be sure that you have understood the law or that you appreciate what the question requires.	Work on your ability to express your ideas in clear and simple language. Check whether your work makes sense by reading aloud to see if the words flow naturally. Get others to read and comment on the clarity of your work so that you can develop a stronger style before the exam. Read your own work through in the exam to check that it is clear.
Lack of analysis	An imbalance between description and analysis in essays written in exams is one of the commonest reasons for weak marks.	Make sure that you understand the difference between description and analysis. Make sure that your revision prepares you to discuss the law as well as describe it and that you tailor the content of your answers to fit the line of analysis required by the question.

▶

Inaccuracy or lack of understanding	An inability to provide an accurate account of the law is an obvious problem in exams as one of their key objectives is to test your understanding of the law.	Revise carefully, building up your knowledge in increments to make sure that you have understood the law. Avoid revision topics that you find to be over-complicated unless there is no choice other than to answer a question on that particular topic. Present clear and simple statements of the law to ensure that your explanations are understood by the examiner.
Problems with written style	Any problems with grammar, punctuation and spelling that appear in coursework will have a negative impact on your exam performance.	Look at your coursework to discover what particular words or punctuation it is that you seem to misuse and find out how to correct this. You may find study support facilities at your university particularly useful in providing help with this sort of problem.
Missing or ineffective application	The greatest weakness in answers to problem questions is lack of application of the law to the facts. If you have not mastered this in your coursework, it is likely that it will be a struggle in the exam.	Practise before the exam to ensure that you get the hang of looking for specific evidence in the facts that you can use in your answer to demonstrate that the requirements of the law are satisfied. Avoid any 'lazy' application phrases such as 'it is clear/obvious that this is established'.
Failure to answer the question	This means that you have presented some relevant law in your answer but that you did not do enough to tailor it to the question and, as such, the general topic has been discussed but the question has not been answered.	Take care to select content that is relevant to the particular question asked, not just to the general topic. Link every significant point back to the question in a clear and specific manner.

No evidence of wider reading	Students sometimes think that research into a topic is only required in coursework. This is not the case. Exam answers will also need to be informed by wider reading.	Incorporate ideas from journal articles into your revision so that they can be used in the exam. Make sure that you can identify the source of your ideas to the examiner.
Not enough case law or ineffective use of case law	Case law is important as a source of legal principle and as an example of the law in operation. Lack of case law or an inability to use case law effectively will weaken answers produced in the exam.	Ensure that case law has a prominent role in your revision so that you are able to remember relevant cases in the exam. If necessary, seek guidance in using case law more effectively.

www.pearsoned.co.uk/lawexpress

■ To find out more ...

Visit the Companion Website where you will find a list of marking criteria that has been tailored to reflect the important features of an exam answer. Use this to evaluate your own practice answers. You can also try it with answers provided on the Companion Website and compare your opinion on the answer to the evaluation of an examiner.

NOTES

NOTES

Appendix

By using this book, you should have found a whole variety of tips and techniques to make your revision more effective and maximise your chances of exam success.

Of these, organisation is one of the most crucial: proper planning prevents poor performance! In this Appendix you will find some checklists that may be useful in reminding you of things to do in the lead up to the exams. Of course, these lists are not exhaustive: if, as you read, there are particular 'don't forget' items that will be useful for you, then add them in. Similarly, if there are points that are listed here that do not work for you, then cross them out. The most important point is making sure that you approach your revision and exams in a structured way and these checklists provide a useful start point for organising your activities.

Exam checklists

■ During the course

- ■ Put the exam dates in your diary
- ■ Organise your revision plan
- ■ Ensure that you have no commitments that clash with the exam
- ■ Collect module information (syllabus, assessment criteria)
- ■ Find past papers and any commentary on past papers
- ■ Consider whether to form a study group
- ■ Start making revision notes
- ■ Work out your particular individual learning profile
- ■ Consider making quizzes or flashcards, etc.
- ■ Consider buying a revision guide

■ One month before the exam

- ■ Check that you know where the exam is, and how you will get there
- ■ Make any other necessary arrangements (child care, etc.)
- ■ Plan your revision so that you know what you are doing each day
- ■ Check to make sure that you have all the materials you need during the revision period
- ■ Form a revision group with other students, making sure to balance group revision with individual study

One week before the exam

- Get plenty of sleep
- Condense your notes
- Get your exam bag ready (statute books, if allowed, water, timepiece, pens, student ID card, etc.)
- Programme the examinations emergency number into your phone
- Plan activities that consolidate your understanding rather than trying to learn new topics
- Write practice answers

The day before the exam

- Set at least one alarm clock
- Go to bed at a sensible time
- Reconfirm travel plans and other arrangements
- Prepare exam clothes
- Work steadily to ensure that all the relevant topics are fresh in your mind
- Avoid last-minute panic and do not give into the temptation to squeeze in 'one last topic'
- Check that your statute book is not annotated

On the day

- Check last-minute details
- Leave your valuables at home
- Leave your phone at home, or switched off in your bag
- Double check contents of exam bag and remember to take it with you!
- Try not to overwork your brain prior to the exam
- Avoid other students if this makes you feel stressed
- Do something relaxing like listen to music or taking a walk so that you feel calm before the exam

Index